Valerie Muter is a consultant clinical psychologist at Great
~~mond~~ Street Hospital for Children where she specialises in
~~king~~ with children with both developmental and neurologi-
~~y~~ based learning disorders. She holds an honorary research
~~owship~~ at the Centre for Reading and Language, University of
~~k~~, and has carried out extensive collaborative research into
~~ding~~ development and dyslexia with Professor Margaret
~~owling~~, the UK's leading authority on dyslexia. She was a
~~nsultant~~ psychologist at the Dyslexia Institute (Dyslexia Action)
~~for~~ 20 years.

Dr Helen Likierman is a consultant clinical psychologist working with families and children (from pre-schoolers to older
adolescents) where there are emotional, social, behavioural or
learning concerns. After her psychology degree, she trained and
worked as a teacher of young primary school children before
moving on to clinical training and a PhD on pre-schoolers'
friendships and peer relationships. She worked for many years as
a practising clinical psychologist in the NHS and was a consultant psychologist at the Dyslexia Institute (Dyslexia Action) for
three years. In addition to her current consultant work, she is
the school counsellor at a large co-educational school. She is the
mother of two teenage children, one of whom has specific learning difficulties.

Also available by Dr Valerie Muter
and Dr Helen Likierman:

Prepare Your Child for School
Top Tips for Starting School

DYSLEXIA

A parents' guide to dyslexia, dyspraxia and other learning difficulties

Dr Valerie Muter and

Dr Helen Likierman

Vermilion

LONDON

1 3 5 7 9 10 8 6 4 2

Published in 2008 by Vermilion, an imprint of Ebury Publishing

Ebury Publishing is a Random House Group company

The Random House Group Limited Reg. No. 954009

Addresses for companies within the Random House Group
can be found at www.rbooks.co.uk

A CIP catalogue record for this book is available from the British Library

The Random House Group Limited supports The Forest Stewardship
Council (FSC), the leading international forest certification organisation.
All our titles that are printed on Greenpeace approved FSC certified
paper carry the FSC logo. Our paper procurement policy can
be found at www.rbooks.co.uk/environment

Designed and set by seagulls.net

Printed and bound in Great Britain by
CPI Mackays, Chatham, ME5 8TD

ISBN 9780091923389

Copies are available at special rates for bulk orders. Contact the sales development
team on 020 7840 8487 for more information.

**London Borough
of Barnet**

Askews	Sep-2008
371.9144	£10.99

Contents

Acknowledgements

We are grateful to our editor, Julia Kellaway, for inviting us to write this book and for her continued excellent editing, support and advice.

Professors Maggie Snowling and Charles Hulme have been extremely generous and helpful, enabling us to be as up to date as possible with the research on learning difficulties. We also owe them a huge debt of thanks for their valuable comments on an earlier draft of this book.

Anna Wagstyl, Special Educational Needs Co-ordinator at a London primary school, patiently talked us through the complexities of the special needs system and we are extremely grateful for her wise words and advice.

Dr Richard Lansdown gave generously of his time and made many perceptive comments on an earlier draft, and we are very appreciative.

David Chamberlain drew the illustrations for the handwriting positions, for which we thank him.

We owe a huge thank you to our 'case histories', particularly Jesse Farragher (and her mother, Rachel) and Helen's son Felix Hale, for giving us their perspectives on what it is like to live with a specific learning difficulty.

We would like to thank Helen's long-suffering husband, Julian, for his forbearance, practical help, editorial flair and common sense. We owe him a huge debt.

Finally, we wish to thank the thousands of children with learning difficulties we have worked with over the years. We have used our clinical experience of these children to reach out to the many more out there who are still struggling.

Introduction
Why is My Child Struggling?

Around the age of seven, your child should have settled comfortably into school and be coping with the work. But some children – many children – are already starting to have difficulties that seem surprising. If you are worried or concerned that your child is failing to progress in a way you instinctively feel is right, then this book is for you.

Children struggle at school for many reasons. Sometimes teachers and parents will say about a child who is struggling, 'If only we could find the key to unlock his difficulties, then he'd be away.' But searching for an elusive key can be successful only when all the facts are known. This is often a long and difficult process, but it doesn't need to be. If you ask the right questions and do the right kinds of observations and assessments, you will find the causes of your child's problems – and therefore the solutions as well.

A parent's desire to find out what their child's particular learning problems are is clearly a sensible ambition, but there can be obstacles. Sometimes it seems there is too much information 'out there' on learning difficulties – dyslexia, dyspraxia, dyscalculia, language and attention problems – and this information can seem conflicting or unclear. This is not altogether surprising as even professionals disagree about the definitions, causes and treatment of learning difficulties. The controversies may be picked up by the media, but without clearly defining the issues or even being accurate. The result is often more worry for parents who feel that they may not be doing the right thing by their child or do not know in which direction to go.

In this book we separate fact from fiction. We will take you through the major learning disorders or difficulties (we prefer 'difficulties' though you will hear the two words used interchangeably) so that you can understand them. We will help you spot your child's learning difficulties; and we will show you what more you need to find out, how to approach your child's school and how to get professional help. Finally, we will give you guidelines, based on our own clinical experience and practice, to what you can do to help your child at home.

Our book is based on the most up-to-date research and practice, on facts and evidence rather than 'old wives' tales' and myths. We draw on research and our own extensive clinical experience (which between us spans around 60 years and thousands of children) to suggest the most effective strategies. The book is for parents of children aged between 7 and 14. These are the most important years for catching problems and helping children overcome them, but obviously the earlier the better.

Step One is to find out whether your child has dyslexia or another learning difficulty – or whether there's nothing too much to worry about. We ask you to start by looking in detail at the problems he or she seems to be having now, and then to look back at your child's early development. We have devised a series of 'checks' for you to try out with your child to test out your hypothesis (belief, feeling, hunch) that he or she could have a learning difficulty.

Step Two gives you lots of ideas about how to approach professionals and to understand how they can help your child. Chapter 7 explains the steps you need to take to get help from school. The education support system is complicated, but it will help you to know the details so you can make sure your child gets the best help possible. Chapter 8 covers what you need to know about making contact with other professionals. In particular, we take you in detail through the psychological assessment as this is so helpful for the understanding of an individual child's difficulties and needs.

Step Three will guide you through all the things you can do at home to help your child. Chapter 10 shows you how you can help a child with dyslexia (improve reading, spelling and written work), with dyspraxia (improve handwriting), with dyscalculia (improve maths) and with SLI (improve language). Chapter 11 gives you strategies for dealing with attention, homework, revising for exams, getting organised and staying motivated.

Throughout the book we draw on our own experience with a number of case histories. We start with an example. Nicholas (not his real name) is a child who came to us for assessment because he was 'struggling with reading at school'. Have you ever said the same about your child? This is his story as told by his mother.

Nicholas

When I look back, Nicholas was such a bright and happy little boy. His dad and I could never have imagined before he started school that he would go on to have so many problems. Nicholas went to our local nursery school at age three – he was so keen to go. He loved it. He liked his teachers, he enjoyed playing with the other children and he found the games and puzzles great fun. His teachers said that he settled in well – they all loved him. And they said that he was so bright, that he'd do well when he started school. And he seemed to get off to a good start. He loved story time, 'show and tell' and learning about numbers. I suppose we first became a little worried when Nicholas seemed a bit slow at learning his letters. But his teacher said not to worry, that some children did get off to a slow start but usually caught up by the end of Reception. The problem was that he didn't catch up by the end of Reception. I said to his teacher, 'Nicholas knows only five letters of the alphabet, yet I can see that his classmates know many more.' 'Let's see how he gets on in Year 1,' she said.

Well, Year 1 came, and Nicholas enjoyed school, liked being with his friends and seemed to be doing fine with his maths. But he hated reading – he wouldn't look at books at home. He'd say, 'Reading is rubbish,' though he still liked being read to. I had a chat with his class teacher and she said, 'Yes, he is a bit slow getting going with his reading. I'll get our classroom assistant to do some extra work with him on his letters and send some books home for him to read with you – I'm sure that will help.' Only it didn't! Nicholas refused to read even the simple story books his teacher sent home. If I pressed him he'd throw them on the floor and have a temper tantrum. I couldn't believe how my lovely, easy-going little pre-schooler was turning into a rather miserable child with an awful temper. And I was shocked to realise that, at the end of Year 1, Nicholas still knew only five letters of the alphabet, while all the other children in his class knew them all. His class teacher was getting worried too – she promised that in Year 2 the special needs co-ordinator would start giving him extra reading lessons.

It's amazing how quickly your child's primary school years speed by. And it's frightening when you have a child like Nicholas who just doesn't 'get' reading at all. Over the next three years, he continued to make very slow progress. He still seemed bright, his maths was good (when he could actually read the question), he liked sports and spending time with his friends. Actually, it was hard to keep close tabs on how Nicholas was getting on with his reading because he flatly refused to read at home. And he usually 'forgot' to bring home his spelling lists. When he did remember, and I was able to bribe him to try and learn the spellings, he could sometimes struggle through the Friday test (getting about half of them right), but he'd have forgotten them all by the next week. I'd talk to his teachers from time to time, but I felt that I was being labelled a 'bit of a nuisance' and a 'neurotic mother'. His teacher would say, 'Don't worry – he's having extra help. He'll be fine – he should catch up in the end.'

By the time Nicholas was 10 years old and in Year 5, I wondered how on earth he was going to cope when he moved to his secondary school. He still couldn't read and made mistakes even when spelling three-letter words. His moods and his refusal to do any homework were driving me mad. His teachers also started to complain that his difficult behaviour was disrupting the class, and they felt he could do the work if he tried harder and concentrated more because they considered him to be a bright boy.

Then a friend of mine suggested that I get Nicholas assessed by a psychologist. I thought this could be a step in the right direction. The psychologist saw Nicholas and then talked to me. 'Did you know that Nicholas has dyslexia?' she said. I didn't, but it felt such a relief to hear that he had a problem I could at last put a name to. She showed me a piece of his writing, and between the two of us we had real difficulty following it because his spelling was so odd.

One day there Bears lee there Pore to cool and, a gill called gould ant the pore and then aet on the cah is the Bard yunh the Beast and then their the beds the Bany Bed oras the Beast, and seh fell a sleß and the Bans tall her off.

The psychologist said, 'I'll talk to his teachers, write a report and make some suggestions about how best to teach him.' So the teachers started to give him more help and put him on a special reading programme. The psychologist put me in touch with the local dyslexia association and I was able to get a lot of advice and support from them.

Nicholas himself is happy to know that his difficulties are not his fault, and that many others share his problems. I just wish I had been able to recognise the problems earlier on. We could have done much more – and Nicholas wouldn't be so far behind and so frustrated and moody. But I'm feeling more positive now, and so is Nicholas. We still have a long way to go – but Nicholas, his dad and me, and his teachers have made a start. And we have the very real feeling that at last we know where we're going.

Nicholas's – and his parents' – problems are not unusual. But we want to make sure that difficulties like his are spotted early, so that effective action can be taken. That's what this book is all about.

So now it's time to deal with your own child's experiences and sort out any concerns you might have. We ask you to think about your concerns now, and then to think about those early days when, perhaps, you might have started to feel just a bit worried. Even if you believe your child has difficulties in only one area, it's worth checking the others too – very many children have more than one problem, and additional problems can easily be missed.

step one

Finding Out

1

Could Your Child Have Dyslexia?

To explain what dyslexia actually is has proved to be quite a challenge, as there are so many different views about how it should be defined. What everyone agrees is that children with dyslexia have much greater difficulty learning to read and spell than would be expected. (This is exactly the difficulty Nicholas had, see page 3.)

Research has shown that almost all children with dyslexia have difficulty with what they hear, not with what they see. Dyslexia is *not* a form of word blindness. What can be said with certainty is that children with dyslexia have a problem with an aspect of spoken language known as **phonological processing.**

Having phonological processing difficulties means that children find it hard to make sense of the speech sounds in words; for example, they cannot easily break a spoken word like 'stop' into its separate sounds 's' – 't' – 'o' – 'p'. Nor can they easily put sounds together (known as blending) – if they hear s-t-o-p, they cannot tell that it makes the spoken word 'stop'. Children need these phonological skills to be able to learn the relationship between sounds and lettters and then to read and spell.

The part played by **intelligence (IQ)** has been a cause of confusion because dyslexia can affect children of almost any ability level. It's a myth that only children with high intelligence have dyslexia. On a practical level it is helpful to recognise that children with dyslexia have literacy levels that are *out of keeping with* their ability level (or IQ) – and possibly also out of keeping with other skills and attainments, such as maths, music or art. For this reason, dyslexia is sometimes referred to as a **specific**

learning difficulty (you might also come across **specific reading** or **specific spelling difficulty**).

Children with below-average intelligence would not be expected to read at a level in keeping with their age. However, there are some lower-ability children who have more difficulty with learning to read than they have in the learning of other skills. Such children should equally be described as having dyslexia (though it needs to be recognised that their low IQ might make *many* aspects of learning a struggle for them).

Of course, not all literacy problems are due to a specific (or even a general) learning difficulty. Some children may progress poorly in reading because they have problems with their schooling – whether as a result of absence due to illness, poor teaching, lack of interest in learning (poor motivation), behaviour problems or attention difficulties. However, in this chapter we are looking at children whose literacy difficulties are a result of the specific learning problem that is dyslexia.

Dyslexia should not be seen as something one either has or doesn't have, but rather a difficulty somewhere along a **continuum** from mild through to severe. Children with *mild* dyslexia may escape major reading problems, but have difficulties with spelling and expressing themselves fluently in writing. Children with *severe* dyslexia will have reading, spelling and writing difficulties that are likely to continue into their adult years.

DYSLEXIA QUIZ

Find out how much you already know – or think you know – about dyslexia in general. Read each statement and circle TRUE or FALSE then look at the following pages for the answers and more information.

1. Dyslexia is more common among boys than girls.

TRUE or FALSE

2. Many children who develop dyslexia have had early (preschool) speech and language problems.   TRUE or FALSE

3. You can tell children have dyslexia from the type of spelling errors they make.   TRUE or FALSE

4. Dyslexia is more common among left-handed than right-handed children.   TRUE or FALSE

5. All children with dyslexia have exceptional talents.

TRUE or FALSE

6. Children with dyslexia are usually clumsy. TRUE or FALSE

7. A child with no reading problems cannot have dyslexia.

TRUE or FALSE

8. Many children with dyslexia may overcome their reading difficulties by their early teenage years.   TRUE or FALSE

9. Playing games like 'I Spy' with letter sounds can help young children with dyslexia.   TRUE or FALSE

dren with dyslexia. TRUE
9. Playing games like 'I Spy' with letter sounds can help young chil-
cult ies by their early teenage years. TRUE
8. Many children with dyslexia may overcome their reading diffi-
7. A child with no reading problems cannot have dyslexia. FALSE
6. Children with dyslexia are usually clumsy. FALSE
5. All children with dyslexia have exceptional talents. FALSE
children. FALSE
4. Dyslexia is more common among left-handed than right-handed
they make. FALSE
3. You can tell children have dyslexia from the type of spelling errors
speech and language problems. TRUE
2. Many children who develop dyslexia have had early (pre-school)
1. Dyslexia is more common among boys than girls. TRUE
Now how did you do?

If you got between 7 and 9 of the quiz items correct, well done – you are aware of many of the important facts. However, it wouldn't be surprising if you didn't score as highly as this, given all the controversy surrounding the subject. By the end of this chapter you should have a clear understanding of what dyslexia is and whether it might be your child's problem.

FACTS ABOUT DYSLEXIA

Many famous people have dyslexia

There is a common myth that children with dyslexia have an exceptional talent or gift, such as in art, design, music or maths. Alas, there is almost no scientific evidence for this. However, having dyslexia does not mean that an individual may not be talented and successful. There are many prominent people with dyslexia. These include Sir Richard Branson (entrepreneur, businessman and adventurer), Ruby Wax (television personality), Lord Richard Rogers (architect), A.A. Gill (journalist), Susan Hampshire (actress) and Sir Steve Redgrave (sportsman). *Every* child has strengths as well as weaknesses – and this is as true for the child with dyslexia as any other. In all cases, it is important for teachers and parents to look for and foster a child's emerging strengths, talents and interests. This is necessary not just for helping with learning in the classroom but also for promoting confidence and self-esteem.

Dyslexia is common

Studies of very large numbers of children can tell us how common learning difficulties are. Different studies do tend to come up with slightly different estimates – it depends on how the learning difficulty is *measured* and how *severe* the problem has to be to count as a difficulty. A working figure for *severe* dyslexia is around 5 per cent, and around 10 per cent if mild difficulties are included. Therefore, far from being rare, dyslexia is indeed a common learning problem. Boys are much more likely to have dyslexia than girls – three boys to every one girl.

Dyslexia runs in families

Dyslexia is a learning difficulty that is largely inherited but in quite a complex way as several genes are involved. Family members often have sets of genes in common and therefore there is a strong risk that dyslexia will pass down through families. Parents (or other close family members) who had difficulty with reading, spelling and writing and struggled in school could well have had dyslexia even if, sadly, their difficulties went unrecognised.

Professor Margaret Snowling, a leading authority on dyslexia, studied children born into families where one parent had dyslexia, and followed them from the age of 3 to 13 years. The aim was to find out more about what causes dyslexia and what puts children *at risk* for reading difficulties. One of the findings was that the risk of dyslexia is very strong in families with a history of reading problems. By the time these at-risk children reached the age of 13 years, an extremely high number – nearly 50 per cent – were experiencing literacy difficulties. So, if you or your partner (or even your or your partner's parents or brothers or sisters) had, or still have, difficulties with literacy then your children are certainly at risk. Of course, it does not mean that your children will definitely have dyslexia, but the *probability* of them having dyslexia is much higher than for other children.

If your child is at risk of an inherited learning difficulty, it would be a very good idea to check it out. Knowing your child is at risk may help you understand where your child's problems are coming from so you can take positive action. In Professor Snowling's study, many parents realised that slowness in learning the alphabet would make learning to read harder, so they spent more time teaching their children letters and their sounds.

Dyslexia causes trouble with reading and spelling

The explanation of dyslexia we gave earlier points to children with dyslexia having phonological problems. Why is this awareness of speech sounds in words, and being able to remember them easily, so important for learning to read? It is because the ability to break up words into their component sounds and to remember the sequence (or order) of sounds are both needed for children to work out what a printed word says. This process is known as decoding – and is what **phonics** is all about. Being able to decode is essential for learning to read and spell. Children with dyslexia are poor at decoding and so are going to find reading and spelling very hard.

Pre-schoolers who understand sounds in words show this by playing games like clapping the syllables or 'beats' in a word; for instance, two claps for dustbin (dust – bin), three claps for umbrella (um – bre – lla). They have fun with nursery rhymes and even make up little rhymes of their own – even if it's only like 'I've been to the loo – poo, poo, poo!' They join in games like 'I Spy'. Parents of children with dyslexia may well recall that their child, when young, had difficulty with these sorts of language games.

Quite a lot of children who go on to have dyslexia have also been late to start talking and may well have had unclear speech. In the research described above, children from families with dyslexia were found to be behind on several aspects of language when they were age three to four (they had less good vocabulary and were more likely to make grammatical errors when they talked). So, both early difficulties with speech and language and difficulties with awareness of speech sounds should be seen as warning signs of possible dyslexia.

As children get a little older – at around the ages of four and five – their understanding of sounds in words becomes greater. Now they are able to think of and say back to you lots of words that begin with the same sound, such as sun, sandwich and sock. They may even be able to 'take away' sounds from words, such as 'sat' without the 'ss' sound says 'at'. They also begin to learn and to remember the sounds or names of the letters of the alphabet. Children with dyslexia find all of these skills very difficult.

Because children with dyslexia have difficulties with speech sounds and with learning alphabet letters from a very early age, it follows that it is possible to 'screen' children for dyslexia as they start school. Indeed, there are tests used by psychologists and teachers that use speech sound and letter games to assess if children aged five are at risk for dyslexia. This is why it is not necessary to wait until the age of seven, when children would normally be reading, to recognise them as certainly having dyslexia. Another type of test used to identify children with dyslexia is a test of nonsense word reading. Nonsense words like 'frod' and 'preet' can only be read by decoding or 'sounding the letters out'. Real words can be recognised, and so read, more easily because they may be familiar or easier to pick up in the context of a story. Children with dyslexia who have very poor decoding skills find it especially hard to read nonsense words.

Problems with spelling

Children with dyslexia usually have even more difficulty with spelling than they do with reading. Even if they overcome their reading problems (and many do by the time they are at secondary school) they are left with continuing and sometimes severe spelling problems. Interestingly, it's not possible to tell if a child has dyslexia by the types of spelling errors seen in their written work. Their spelling mistakes look exactly like those made by younger children rather than being of a different kind.

Problems with reading comprehension

Are children with decoding or reading accuracy problems also poor at reading comprehension (that is, understanding and remembering what they read)? This is a really important issue because the goal of reading is to understand and take on board what has been read. Children who read the words and sentences without understanding are sometimes described by teachers as 'barking at print'. Children's ability to understand what they read will depend on the number of words they can recognise. So a child with severe dyslexia who is able to read only very few words is likely to have problems with reading comprehension. The child with mild dyslexia who has a bigger reading vocabulary would be expected to have less of a problem with comprehension. Indeed, some children with mild dyslexia understand well what they read. These children usually have an above-average IQ and, most importantly, good spoken-language skills. They are therefore able to use their good vocabulary and the clues given by the context of the words in the story to help them make even better sense of what they read. If children have reading comprehension problems, it is important not just to assess how accurate their reading is, but also to look at their language skills. Children who find it hard to understand spoken language and who have a limited spoken vocabulary will also have problems understanding what they read.

Dyslexia is not caused by left-handedness

Some people believe that dyslexia is caused by being left-handed or crossed- or mixed-lateral (for example, being right-handed but left-eyed). There is no evidence for these conditions being related to dyslexia. Nor is there any evidence that being forced to change handedness (a naturally left-handed child being made to write with the right hand) will cause that child to develop dyslexia. It might, however, lead to handwriting problems and lack of confidence or even emotional distress.

Children with dyslexia have problems remembering speech sounds

Problems with another skill – short-term memory for speech sounds – also affect many children with dyslexia. Children who have been late to talk are especially likely to have problems with short-term verbal memory. You may have noted how difficult it is for your child to remember instructions even when he or she seems to be paying attention and listening carefully. Your child's short-term verbal memory can be assessed by psychologists or teachers by getting him or her to repeat sequences of words or sentences or strings of numbers.

Are there different types of dyslexia?

This is another area where there is much disagreement. The most usual view is that there is only one type of dyslexia: phonological processing and decoding problems are the cause of reading difficulties. The underlying cause is the same for all children with dyslexia – it's just that some have more severe difficulties than others.

A rather different view of dyslexia is that there are two subtypes – phonological dyslexia and surface dyslexia. Children with phonological dyslexia have severe reading and spelling problems that are caused by their phonological processing and decoding difficulties. Children with surface dyslexia have fewer phonological processing and decoding problems; but they are likely to have other difficulties, for instance with short-term verbal memory. Children with surface dyslexia usually catch up in their reading accuracy after a slow start, but they often continue to have reading speed and spelling problems.

What these views have in common is that they describe dyslexia as due to an underlying spoken language difficulty. If phonological and surface dyslexia were really found to be two completely separate learning problems, then in theory no one child could move from one subtype to the other. In practice, however, a child can go from showing the profile of phonological dyslexia to resembling a child with surface dyslexia, if over time they receive good tuition in phonological processing and decoding. More evidence is needed to decide for sure which of these views – one type or two subtypes – best describes dyslexia.

There is also the issue of visual- versus sound-based dyslexia. Most research suggests that visual skills play only a small part in learning to read and spell. It is only very occasionally that a child with literacy problems is found to have visual processing difficulties of one kind or another, but without having any phonological and decoding difficulties.

Children with dyslexia often have other difficulties too

A high number of children with dyslexia have other significant learning difficulties too. This is known as co-occurrence or co-morbidity. These other learning difficulties are persistent language problems; motor and nonverbal difficulties, including clumsiness; maths problems; and attention problems.

The at risk study showed that around 70 per cent of children with dyslexia had one or more of these other learning problems as well. Many children with dyslexia have problems with maths because dyslexia affects the verbal aspects of number processing.

They find it hard to learn the number names so they count slowly and make mistakes when doing calculations. They also find it hard to recall maths facts like multiplication tables. There are also many children with dyslexia (at least 35 per cent) who have attention problems.

There is growing evidence that dyslexia is not quite the very specific or selective difficulty that it was once thought to be. This is not just because there may be different subtypes of dyslexia, but also because other (co-occurring) learning difficulties have such a marked effect on how the dyslexia shows itself. It is, therefore, vital to recognise all the difficulties shown by a child with dyslexia so that these can be dealt with alongside help given for the literacy problems. How to recognise these other problems will be described in Chapters 2, 3, 4 and 5.

Not all children with dyslexia fail to read – but dyslexia affects educational progress

Many children with dyslexia will indeed have reading problems, either mild or severe. Small numbers of children with dyslexia escape reading difficulties but still have problems with learning to spell and to write. Many issues affect how well children with dyslexia are likely to manage by the time they leave school:

■ How **severe** the dyslexia is will have a large effect on how well children can benefit from teaching. Children with a severe degree of dyslexia (very poor phonological processing and decoding skills) are likely to have long-term and fairly marked reading, spelling and writing difficulties. Children with mild dyslexia may well in time overcome all or almost all of their reading problems. They may, however, continue to have difficulties with spelling and written expression – and also speed of reading and writing. Sometimes children with mild dyslexia appear to cope very well in primary and early secondary school, particularly if they have had good learning support. But at GCSE, or sometimes only at A level, they find the demands of the course (including volume of work and working under time pressure) overwhelming, because their speed of reading and writing is slow.

■ Some children with dyslexia appear to make very slow progress in the early stages of learning to read – even those with a lot of learning support. The good news is that many children seem suddenly to 'take off' in reading when they are around 12 to 13 years of age (and some earlier than this). Children with dyslexia seem to need to reach a **threshold** where they are able to make firm links between each speech sound and the letters that represent them. It is then that decoding becomes automatic. This threshold point is reached after lots of practice. Reading then seems to 'click' into place. Parents, teachers and children should definitely not be discouraged if early progress seems to be slow. They should keep on working towards the 'click point'!

■ Taking off in reading during the early teenage years is partly about reaching the click point – but often also about learning to **compensate** for difficulties. To compensate, the child needs to use strengths such as good language and memory skills to get around learning difficulties. Children can be helped to find other routes to achieving a particular goal. So, for example, children with dyslexia who have good language skill may compensate for their poor decoding by using their good vocabulary to fill in the gaps of words that they can only partly decode. Additionally, they can use the structure of the sentence and what's happening in the story to help them read words. While some verbally able children with dyslexia discover ways of compensating for themselves, others need structured help to realise what a difference this can make to their reading skills.

■ The child's **personality** may have a strong effect – children who are determined, motivated and who do not allow themselves to feel negative about their difficulties tend to work harder and keep going for longer. These children will make more progress than those who become demoralised and give up.

■ The age that the difficulties are recognised will make a difference to how well the child progresses. **Early identification** of the problems means that help can be given before the child has fallen too far behind, and before confidence and motivation have been lost.

■ How well children cope depends on whether or not they receive extra or **specialist teaching** – and on the quality and intensity of that teaching, and whether support can be given at all stages of their school life, if need be. How children with dyslexia can best be taught and supported at school is covered briefly on page 32 and more fully in Chapter 7.

■ How well children get on depends not only on the help given at school but also on **how much parents are able to do at home** (see Chapters 10 and 11 for the many things that parents can do to help).

■ Children with **only** dyslexia to deal with are likely to do better than those who have additional (**co-occurring**) problems.

■ Children who are brought up learning a **second language** and who have dyslexia in addition will probably find learning to read (English, but maybe the other language too) even more difficult. For the child who does not have dyslexia, learning two languages is generally an advantage – not just culturally and socially but also because it helps them appreciate the phonology and grammar of the languages they speak.

■ Children who develop **negative views** about their own achievements and abilities can become turned off learning and even school in general. Such children may be seen as a 'behaviour problem' because they refuse or fail to do their work, bunk off school (usually the older ones) and argue with teachers and parents. Children who are motivated and have good self-esteem will do better academically.

To find out whether your child might have dyslexia, first complete the General Questionnaire below to look at how well your child is progressing in literacy now. Next, think back to your child's early years to complete the Early Signs Questionnaire that follows. At the end of each questionnaire look at the results to see whether or not there are signs that your child has dyslexia. When you have all this information from the questionnaires, you can follow up your concerns using our Dyslexia Checks for your child's age group (either 7–11 or 12–14, see page 24).

GENERAL QUESTIONNAIRE: COULD YOUR CHILD HAVE DYSLEXIA?

1. Do you feel that your child is not achieving at school as well as he/she should?
Yes, definitely ❏   Yes, somewhat ❏   No ❏

2. Is he/she struggling with reading?
Yes, definitely ❏   Yes, somewhat ❏   No ❏

3. Is he/she struggling with spelling and written work?
Yes, definitely ❏   Yes, somewhat ❏   No ❏

4. Does he/she still confuse letters when reading and spelling (especially 'b-d', 'p-q')?
Yes, definitely ❏   Yes, somewhat ❏   No ❏

5. Does he/she find it hard to decode (sound out) new words?
Yes, definitely ❏   Yes, somewhat ❏   No ❏

6. Does he/she confuse words in writing that sound alike but have different meanings and spellings (e.g. 'there/their', 'right/write', 'wear/where')?
Yes, definitely ❏   Yes, somewhat ❏   No ❏

7. Is he/she reluctant to read (to him/herself or to you)?
Yes, definitely ❏   Yes, somewhat ❏   No ❏

8. Does he/she write words that don't look like the word he/she is trying to spell (e.g. hatn for hand, brith for bridge)?
Yes, definitely ❏   Yes, somewhat ❏   No ❏

9. Does he/she have difficulty in remembering lists of items or things to do?
Yes, definitely ❏   Yes, somewhat ❏   No ❏

10. Does he/she worry about school work and feel unconfident in class?
Yes, definitely ❏   Yes, somewhat ❏   No ❏

11. Are there any other members of the family who have had difficulties in reading and/or spelling?
Yes, definitely ❏   Yes, somewhat (distant members) ❏
No ❏

Results: General Questionnaire

If you ticked 'Yes, definitely' for most of the questions, then you have good reason to be concerned that your child might have dyslexia. Do follow up by completing the Dyslexia Check for your child's age group (see page 24).

If you ticked 'Yes, somewhat' for many items, it would also be worth following up with the Dyslexia Check.

If you ticked 'No' for most of the items, then your child's literacy development seems to be progressing well.

Now think back to your child's early years.

EARLY SIGNS QUESTIONNAIRE

1. Did your child have difficulty learning nursery rhymes?
Yes, definitely ❏   Yes, somewhat ❏   No ❏

2. Did he/she have trouble playing 'I Spy'?

Yes, definitely ❑   Yes, somewhat ❑   No ❑

3. Was he/she late to talk (usual is first few words by 12 months, short two- to three-word phrases by 15–18 months, short but complete sentences by two and a half years)?

Yes, definitely ❑   Yes, somewhat ❑   No ❑

4. Was your child's speech unclear and difficult for others to understand?

Yes, definitely ❑   Yes, somewhat ❑   No ❑

5. Did he/she find it hard to learn the alphabet during the Reception year?

Yes, definitely ❑   Yes, somewhat ❑   No ❑

6. Did he/she enjoy looking at story (not just picture) books with you?

No, not interested ❑   Sometimes interested ❑
Really enjoyed them ❑

7. Did he/she seem to know how books 'work' (i.e. concepts of print):

- that we read from left to right?   Yes ❑   No ❑
- where to find the top and bottom of the page?
                                                       Yes ❑   No ❑
- where the front and back of the book are?   Yes ❑   No ❑
- that the pictures related to the printed text? Yes ❑   No ❑

Results: Early Signs Questionnaire

If, for items 1 to 5, you mostly ticked 'Yes, definitely', then your child as a pre-schooler would have been at risk for dyslexia.

If you mostly ticked 'Yes, somewhat' for items 1 to 5 then your child showed some minor risk factors for dyslexia.

It you mostly ticked 'No' for items 1 to 5 then your child's early pre-reading development was normal.

If, for item 6, you ticked 'No, not interested', and answered mostly 'No' to the questions in item 7, then your child was showing signs of dyslexia from an early age. If you ticked

'Sometimes interested' for item 6 and were unsure whether to answer 'Yes' or 'No' for item 7, then your child was showing early signs of 'possible' dyslexia. If you ticked 'Really enjoyed them' for item 6 and answered mostly 'Yes' for item 7, then your child's early awareness of letters and print was developing well.

YOUR OWN CHECKS

The checks you make yourself will add to the information you have gathered from the questionnaires. The following Dyslexia Checks are based on up-to-date knowledge about the learning difficulties underlying dyslexia. They will show you whether or not your child is experiencing some of the problems typical of children with dyslexia. However, they are only pointers to whether or not a more detailed assessment – of the sort done by a psychologist or specialist teacher using standardised tests – is needed.

Checks for ages 7–11
Writing letters
Ask your child to print clearly the letters of the alphabet in order, first with lower-case letters and then with capital letters.

Score the number of correct letters written: lower case [/26], capitals [/26]. Also note whether your child has put any letters in the wrong order.

Reading words
Ask your child to read these words:

sight	because	know
design	bridge	noise
contraption	rhyming	message
probably		[/10] correct

Reading nonsense words
Ask your child to read (decode) these nonsense words.

drap	misk	smeet
frelps	twump	doslen
kooptus	limdrad	grofmult
shancrell		[/10] correct

Repeating nonsense words
Ask your child to repeat after you each of these nonsense words. Say each word only once and score it incorrect if your child cannot begin to repeat it after one hearing. You should practise reading these words by yourself first. Look at the box overleaf for the correct *pronunciation of the vowels*. Also, do make sure your child is listening before you start the check. Both the pronunciation of each syllable and the order have to be right to score as correct.

moofip	[mōō – fĭp]
chezmong	[chĕz – mŏng]
plashleeguv	[plăsh – lēē – gŭv]
tuvzigop	[tŭv – zĭ –gŏp]
thipundojee	[thĭp – ŭn – dō – jēē]
shavroozepgos	[shăv – rōō – zĕp – gŏs]

[/6] correct

Pronunciation of Vowel Sounds

A straight line above the vowel indicates a 'long' sound.

A u-shaped mark above the vowel indicates that the vowel sound is 'short'.

ā – long sound as in 'ape'
ă – short sound as in 'apple'

ē or ēē – long sound as in 'eel'
ě – short sound as in 'egg'

ī – long sound as in 'ice'
ĭ – short sound as in 'ink'

ō or ōō – long sound as in 'oops'
ŏ – short sound as in 'orange'

ū – long sound as in 'use'
ŭ – short sound as in 'umbrella'

Phonological awareness

Pronunciation of individual letter sounds is actually quite tricky, and many people get it wrong. Look at the box below explaining the problem of 'schwa' sounds and how to avoid them.

Pronouncing Sounds Correctly

When working with letter sounds, it is important to pronounce the consonants as clearly as possible. When pronouncing 'b' and 'm', for example, be careful not to add an 'uh', like 'buh' or 'muh'; this 'uh' sound is called a 'schwa' – it does tend to distort sounds, so keep it to a minimum. Pronouncing the schwa risks turning a word like 'dog' into something like 'duh-o-guh'. The letters 'd' and 'g' need to be pronounced with very short, sharp sounds as they actually sound in the word – 'dd' and 'gg'. The same is true for all the other consonants – 'bb', 'mm', 'ss' and so on.

Ask your child to say the word 'pat'. Now ask him/her to say 'pat' without the 'p' sound (it makes 'at'). Then ask your child to say 'zoom' without the 'm' ('zoo') and 'trip' without the 't' ('rip'). For each example, praise your child for the correct answer. If your child doesn't know or gives the wrong answer tell him/her what it should be. Now try these without giving further help:

Cat without the /c/ says? (at)

Meet without the /t/ says? (me)

Slip without the /s/ says? (lip)

Told without the /d/ says? (toll)

Stick without the /t/ says? (sick)

Smash without the /m/ says? (sash)

Spilt without the /l/ says? (spit)

String without the /r/ says? (sting)

[/8] correct

Results: Checks for ages 7–11
Writing letters
Children aged 7 and above should be able to write all the letters of the alphabet – especially in lower case – easily and accurately.

Reading words
This list of words covers very commonplace words that children should be learning through the years of primary school. Children aged 7 should be able to read at least the top line of words. Children of 8 or 9 should be able to read most of these words, with perhaps just two or three errors. Children of 10 and 11 should be able to read them all without difficulty.

Reading nonsense words

Children as young as 5 learn to decode simple three-letter nonsense words like 'fap'. Between the ages of 7 and 9, children whose reading is developing normally should be able to decode one-syllable nonsense words, while children of 10 to 11 should be able to decode the two-syllable nonsense words as well.

Repeating nonsense words

By the time children are 11, they should be able to repeat correctly all of these without difficulty. However, children between 7 and 8 might be expected to make a few errors.

Phonological awareness

These 'take away' sound tests are good at picking up whether a child has phonological awareness difficulties that lead to problems with decoding. Children of 7 should be able to manage easily taking away beginning and end sounds. Children from 8 to 11 should also be able to manage the middle sounds.

Checks for ages 12–14

And now the checks for teenagers. Of course, you need to explain to your child why you are doing this. By this stage, hopefully, you and your child will have talked about any problems with school work. These checks to find out more about your child's difficulties should be presented to him/her as being helpful for finding a positive way forwards.

Spelling words

Ask your teenager to write the following words; read them aloud to him/her one at a time and repeat the word if you need to.

design	where	lazier
cough	shouldn't	switched
ceiling	horrible	addition
fountain		

Spelling nonsense words

Ask him/her to spell some nonsense words. Read them out one at a time, repeating if necessary and having first checked your pronunciation of the vowels from the box on page 26. Acceptable spellings are given below – all are based on standard, regular spelling rules.

Nonsense words (with pronunciation guide)	*Acceptable spellings*
pīming	piming (or pyming or pieming) but *not* pimming
fŏtched	fotched (or foched)
quĭstly	quistly (or kwistly)
glăcked	glacked (or glact) but *not* glackt, glakt, glaked or glaced
twŭmple	twumple (or twumpul) but *not* twumpull
shĕmsert	shemsert (or shemsurt)
tŏlsmid	tolsmid (or tollsmid)
sprōde	sprode (or sproad or sprowed)

Phonological awareness

Ask him/her to say some words backwards – where the first and last letter sounds have to be swapped. For example, you say 'pat', and he/she should say 'tap' (give this example to get started).

Now try these:

You say	*Correct answer*
pool	loop
lease	seal
chip	pitch
but	tub

Now, to make this harder, tell your child that next you will say a nonsense word that when repeated backwards will make a real word. Again, practise yourself before you start. It is really important to point out that your child should concentrate on the *sounds* he/she hears and not think of the spelling.

You say	*Correct answer*	
ēēm	me	
ōōsh	shoo	
găt	tag	
lēēts	steel	
pĭlc(k)	clip	
nŭps	spun	[/10] correct

Results: Checks for ages 12–14
Spelling words
Youngsters of this age should be able to write these common words without making mistakes.

Spelling nonsense words
The same is true for these nonsense words.

Phonological awareness

Problems saying words backwards will help pick up if your child has difficulties with phonological awareness. It is harder than taking away a sound (given for the 7–11 checks), but should be managed by the early teenage years. Also, saying words backwards that go from nonsense to real is harder than going from real to real, and quite a few 12–14 year olds (and even older) might find this tricky.

THE WAY FORWARD

Identifying dyslexia

If, after completing the questionnaires and checks, you feel that your child may have dyslexia, talk to the teachers about further assessment and what extra teaching might be needed.

Nicholas, continued

Looking again at the case of Nicholas, the results of the tests he was given showed how his struggles with work were in fact due to dyslexia.

Nicholas was 10 years old when his mother brought him for an assessment. The main concern, as she saw it, was his great difficulty in learning to read. He seemed bright so why couldn't he learn and remember printed words? The first test Nicholas was given was a test of general ability or IQ (see Chapter 8 for a fuller description of these sorts of tests). He achieved a verbal (or language-based) IQ of 115, well above the national average of 100 and in the top 20 per cent for his age group. His nonverbal IQ (based on puzzle and pattern-based materials) was 105, which was comfortably average. These findings certainly confirmed Nicholas's mother's impression that her son was indeed bright.

But Nicholas appeared to have some 'block' in learning to read. He was asked to read out loud some short prose passages – he scored in the bottom 2 per cent for his age group. On a spelling test he scored in the bottom 8 per cent. Yet his maths, though not brilliant, was much better than his literacy skills – just slightly below expectation in fact. Nicholas's very severe underachievement in reading and spelling relative to his other abilities and skills suggested that he might have dyslexia. Tests of underlying skills confirmed this to be the case. Nicholas was first given a test in which he had to delete (or 'take away') a sound from each of 24 nonsense words to get to a real word (for instance, 'dreep' without the 'r' says 'deep'). Nicholas got 4 correct, when for his age group he should have scored 17 correct. Next, Nicholas was given a test of nonsense word reading. He struggled to read even the very simple three-letter nonsense words like 'fep'. He read 2 out of 20 correctly, while other children of his age would be expected to read easily 14 or 15 of these correctly. It was clear that Nicholas had phonological processing and decoding difficulties typical of children with dyslexia – and this was why he was having so much trouble learning to read and spell.

Nicholas was very aware of his struggles at school. His mother filled in a behaviour checklist, and Nicholas scored in the 'clinical problem' range for 'anxious/depressed' and 'attention problems'. He was very poorly motivated to read. When he was asked what sort of things he liked to read, he replied, 'None.' When asked if he could name two or three of his favourite authors, he responded, 'Don't know any.'

The psychologist's report stated that Nicholas had dyslexia and recommended specialist teaching programmes. His mother shared this with his teachers, and Nicholas was given one-to-one literacy support that was backed up by a home programme.

Teaching works

Much is now known about teaching children with dyslexia, which is good news, but specialist teaching is needed for children to make good progress. What is offered in the classroom will usually be insufficient for the child with moderate to severe dyslexia. The main parts of a specialist teaching programme need to be:

■ **Phonological awareness training.** Children should be taught to analyse and process speech sounds in words. This can be done through games like 'I Spy', rhyming and 'taking away sounds' (see page 27). When children improve in their phonological awareness they will be able to move on to a phonic teaching programme.

■ **Instruction in phonics.** This should take the form of a systematic and step-by-step programme that helps children learn to decode – that is, to build up written words from sounds (spelling) and to break down printed words into sounds (reading). Children with marked dyslexia will need intensive (even daily) teaching and much practice to get these phonic skills in place – but it can be done. And once the phonics take off there will be a big improvement in reading and spelling.

For older children a wider range of literacy skills will need to be taught too, and these are covered in Chapters 7 and 10.

■　■　■

Dyslexia is a real, definable problem that affects many children. It is a specific, not a general, learning difficulty. Some children with dyslexia will have reading, writing and spelling problems, while others will have only writing and spelling problems. What they have in common is a difficulty with phonological processing (an inability to make sense of speech sounds). Action needs to be taken to prevent children from falling further and further behind their classmates. Knowing who is at risk (coming from a family with dyslexia or being late to talk or being slow to learn the alphabet letters) should trigger early action. Specialist teaching is needed for good progress in reading and spelling.

If you suspect that your child has dyslexia, do follow this up by talking to your child's teachers (see Chapter 7). There is also much that you can do to help at home with your child's literacy skills (Chapter 10) and motivation to learn (Chapter 11).

2

Could Your Child Have Dyspraxia?

Dyspraxia is a problem of **motor co-ordination.** Children with dyspraxia have poor motor (physical movement) skills that are not in line with their other abilities or in keeping with what would be expected for their age. The problems will interfere either with academic achievements (like handwriting and drawing) or with daily life activities (such as dressing and sport) or both.

Like dyslexia, dyspraxia is a **specific** or **selective learning difficulty**. The child with dyspraxia has a difficulty with either or both of the following:

- **Gross motor co-ordination** – this means difficulties in co-ordinating whole or large body movements. Children are likely to be poor at many sports (especially ball games) and are often seen as 'clumsy'.
- **Fine motor co-ordination** – this means difficulty in co-ordinating finger and hand movements that are needed for handwriting, drawing, eating and dressing.

Understanding dyspraxia can be very confusing because so many terms have been used – and they keep changing! Children have been labelled with 'clumsy child syndrome', 'right-brain disorder' and 'nonverbal learning difficulty'. The term that is most favoured now is **developmental co-ordination disorder (DCD)**, and in the US **nonverbal learning difficulty (NVLD)** has run a close second. Do all these different labels mean the same thing? Well, roughly, they do. Having said that, nonverbal learning difficulties seems to imply a wider range of difficulties beyond motor – for instance, difficulties in understanding visual and spatial relationships which would, for instance, make it hard for children to do jigsaw puzzles, make sense of maps and draw their way out of a maze. Sometimes children with NVLD have social difficulties too. We feel that the term used to describe an individual child's problems should reflect the type of difficulties the child is showing – so dyspraxia or DCD for those with mainly motor problems and NVLD for children with mainly perceptual and spatial difficulties. Mostly we will use 'dyspraxia' as the general term.

As with dyslexia, dyspraxia is not an all-or-nothing problem. Rather, the difficulties fall along a **continuum** ranging from mild through to severe. Some children's difficulties may be so mild as to have little impact on their day-to-day lives, whereas for children with severe dyspraxia the problems have major disrupting effects on their classroom performance, and well beyond. It is perfectly possible for children to have dyspraxia and yet be good at sport; these children will have good gross motor skills that enable them to kick a football or play tennis, but weak fine motor skills that may cause problems with, for instance, handwriting in the classroom. Some children even do very well learning musical instruments – though the mechanics sometimes take a little longer to achieve.

Dyspraxia can also be used as a term to describe some children who have a certain kind of speech difficulty. This is sometimes called 'verbal dyspraxia', although many speech and language therapists now prefer the term **childhood apraxia of speech**. The child has unclear speech caused by difficulties in moving lips, tongue and palate in a co-ordinated way.

DYSPRAXIA QUIZ

How much do you know about dyspraxia? Read each statement and circle TRUE or FALSE, then look at the following pages for the answers and more information.

1. Dyspraxia occurs equally in boys and girls. TRUE or FALSE

2. Dyspraxia runs in families.   TRUE or FALSE

3. Being left-handed can cause dyspraxia.   TRUE or FALSE

4. Dyspraxia can be caused by emotional problems.

TRUE or FALSE

5. Many children with dyspraxia have attention problems as well.   TRUE or FALSE

6. Being verbally bright can help children deal with and compensate for their dyspraxic difficulties.

TRUE or FALSE

7. Dyspraxia can be easily diagnosed in pre-schoolers.

TRUE or FALSE

8. There are very few effective treatments for dyspraxia.

TRUE or FALSE

9. Children with dyspraxia outgrow their problems by adolescence.   TRUE or FALSE

Now how did you do?

1. Dyspraxia occurs equally in boys and girls. FALSE
2. Dyspraxia runs in families. TRUE
3. Being left-handed can cause dyspraxia. FALSE
4. Dyspraxia can be caused by emotional problems. FALSE
5. Many children with dyspraxia have attention problems as well. TRUE
6. Being verbally bright can help children deal with and compensate for their dyspraxic difficulties. TRUE
7. Dyspraxia can be easily diagnosed in pre-schoolers. FALSE
8. There are very few effective treatments for dyspraxia. TRUE
9. Children with dyspraxia outgrow their problems by adolescence. FALSE

If you got between 7 and 9 of the items correct, well done – you have a good understanding of what dyspraxia is. It is often a misunderstood as well as under-recognised learning difficulty – so read on now to get an up-to-date picture of what is known.

FACTS ABOUT DYSPRAXIA

Dyspraxia is common

There aren't as many studies showing how common dyspraxia is as there are for dyslexia. However, from a good recent population study, it seems that around 5 per cent of children could be considered to have severe dyspraxia/developmental co-ordination disorder, and another 8–9 per cent to have moderate problems. There are many more boys than girls affected – four boys to every girl with severe problems and seven boys to every girl for moderate problems. Dyspraxia is clearly a common learning difficulty. Unfortunately, fewer children than these figures lead one to expect are actually picked up in schools or in clinics. There is therefore good reason to believe that many children's dyspraxic difficulties go unrecognised in the classroom – and these children may well be unfairly labelled as 'lazy' or 'careless', or even be said to have a 'behaviour problem'.

Dyspraxia affects different areas of development

Much less is known about the nature and causes of dyspraxia/DCD than for dyslexia. Dyspraxia is a recognised specific learning difficulty though it doesn't appear to have a standard set of signs, symptoms and underlying difficulties, unlike dyslexia. In dyslexia the underlying difficulty is with phonological (speech sound) processing. However, dyspraxia seems to occur across a number of developmental areas including motor skills, visual perception and spatial ability – and sometimes speech (apraxia of speech) too. This is why one child described as having dyspraxia might have a very different set of problems from another child who also has dyspraxia.

There is an interesting relationship between what the child

'sees' (the visual side) and how his or her body 'responds' (the motor side). Studies of children with dyspraxia show they often have problems with visual tasks that don't require a motor response. For instance, copying or tracing a triangle needs a motor response (the actual drawing). However, asking the child to decide what a shape would *look* like if it were rotated, say, 90 degrees would not need a motor response but would still involve visual perceptual skills. Children with dyspraxia find this rotation task difficult. As vision is necessary to guide motor skills, a 'nonverbal learning difficulties' label is useful because it implies not only motor but also visual and spatial problems. Psychologists making assessments look out for a significantly lower *nonverbal* than *verbal* IQ. Such a discrepancy between the two types of ability is typical of the child with dyspraxia/DCD/NVLD.

Dyspraxia runs in families

What is known about the causes of dyspraxia is that, like dyslexia, dyspraxia often runs in families. Furthermore, there is evidence from a recent study with twins that dyspraxia does indeed have a genetic basis. (In identical twins where one twin had been found to have dyspraxia, there was a very high chance that the other also showed signs of dyspraxia; whereas for non-identical twins, the likelihood of both twins having dyspraxia was much less.) In addition, it is known that being born prematurely and having a very low birth weight put children at risk for dyspraxia.

Dyspraxia is not caused by left-handedness

It is important to clear up some common myths and confusions about dyspraxia. For example, it has been suggested that dyspraxia is more common in left-handed children. However, this is not true – left-handedness on its own is not a cause of dyspraxia, although learning to write may be more of a challenge in general for left handers than for right handers. For a left hander to be described as having dyspraxia there would have to be motor and perhaps perceptual difficulties too.

Dyspraxia is not caused by emotional difficulties

Some people have suggested that emotional difficulties cause dyspraxia, but this has not been confirmed by good research studies. However, having dyspraxia can create problems not only for children's academic performance but also for their emotional well-being and self-esteem. This would be particularly the case if their dyspraxia has not been recognised – and especially if they have been labelled 'lazy', 'careless' or 'naughty'.

Children with dyspraxia usually have other learning difficulties too

Like dyslexia, dyspraxia commonly co-occurs alongside other learning difficulties (see also Chapter 6). Around half the children with dyspraxia/DCD also show signs of attention difficulties, with roughly 20 per cent having full-blown ADHD (Attention Deficit with Hyperactivity Disorder; see Chapter 4 for an explanation of this form of learning difficulty).

As visual perception/motor and attention difficulties are so commonly found together, a special name has sometimes been given to describe the condition – DAMP (Deficit of Attention and Motor Perception). *Severe* DAMP affects 1–2 per cent of young children. Children with severe DAMP show difficulties with:

- attention
- gross motor skills
- fine motor skills
- visual perception
- and sometimes, speech

A further 3–6 per cent show DAMP in a milder form. More boys than girls are affected, with twice as many boys as girls having DAMP. In the pre-school years, these children are most often seen as hyperactive and inattentive, and it is only later that the perceptual and motor difficulties become evident as the child becomes unwilling to write or draw or has lots of bumps, bruises and accidents.

Dyspraxia/DCD also commonly co-occurs with language

difficulties, reading problems and maths difficulties. In fact, as many as 60 per cent of children with DCD/dyspraxia also have a language impairment (see Chapter 3). More than half the children with dyspraxia/DCD have a reading difficulty (see Chapter 1).

Difficulties with social relationships are often mentioned. Although there are few exact statistics, clinical studies have shown that many children with DCD/dyspraxia do also have problems relating to their peers. One view is that these children find it hard to understand and 'read' nonverbal social cues, such as body posture, facial expression and gestures. Children with poor motor skills may have low self-esteem because they are not performing well academically, nor are they able to shine on the sports field, which can be damaging to self-esteem, especially in boys.

Dyspraxia affects children's education – and everyday life too

The effect of dyspraxia on a child's classroom experience, and indeed life in school generally, can be huge. How much children are affected depends not just on how severe the problem is and how it shows itself, but also on the child's personality and ability to compensate for the difficulties. Children with good language skills will be able to develop ways of compensating for their dyspraxic difficulties by guiding their actions through words, for example, talking their way through a map route. Teachers can also have a big effect on children's ability to cope by showing that they recognise their difficulties and offering both practical help and general support.

Dyspraxia can affect children's learning in the classroom in a number of ways (though, of course, not all will necessarily be present in any one child):

- Very poor, and often illegible, handwriting – this can affect a child's grades, the teacher's view of a child's motivation, and willingness to put pencil to paper.
- Slow speed of writing – work is often not finished and exams not completed within the time limit.

- Poor and messy presentation of written work – this can give an impression of carelessness and lack of effort.
- Difficulties in using equipment such as scissors, rulers, compasses and protractors.
- Difficulty with technical drawings, scientific diagrams, maps and graphs – this can cause problems in geography, science, maths and DT.
- Problems with maths including geometry, symmetry, decimal point placement, aligning columns when setting out sums, understanding areas, perimeters and volumes, setting out of steps in problem-solving exercises.
- Difficulty in organising files and exercise books, poor time-keeping (meeting schedules and deadlines), poor organisation of work space with materials often being lost or misplaced.
- Difficulty copying from the board, especially at speed – children with this problem find it hard to take down notes and to write down assignments and homework tasks.

The effects of dyspraxia can extend beyond the classroom into everyday life, so that children have:

- Difficulties in the morning with dressing – this can result in being late for school or turning up looking scruffy (with shoes on the wrong feet, jumpers back to front, buttons fastened in the wrong holes and ties and shoelaces a constant menace).
- Problems in dressing after sports and gym lessons – so they are late for the next class.
- Feelings of inferiority on the sports field or in the gym – this can lead to being socially isolated and even becoming figures of fun.
- Accidents and risk of injury at home, school or out on the streets.
- Untidy and messy bedrooms.
- Messy eating habits – food dropped on to clothes or the floor (creating more cleaning and washing for adults who

might get annoyed) and difficulty with managing knife and fork, often to the embarrassment of parents, especially when eating out.

■ Difficulties with transport and finding their way around, especially with less-familiar routes – leading to fears of travelling around alone or annoyance at their lack of independence.

Dyspraxia often goes unrecognised

Dyspraxia is arguably the most difficult specific learning problem for parents and teachers to spot. This is because the signs can be interpreted in so many different ways – does the child have a real difficulty or is he or she just lazy and careless or maybe unhappy? Because of this, many children with dyspraxia slip through the net. Also, with very young children, it is hard to know whether their motor problems are likely to be a persisting difficulty or whether they just need a little more time for their nervous systems to mature. However, it is possible to pick up the signs of dyspraxia by asking the right questions of parents and of the older children themselves and also by collecting evidence.

Jesse, aged 14, nearly slipped through the net. Here is her mum's (Rachel's) account.

Jesse

Jesse had sauntered through school without any difficulties until Year 9, when her grades began to slip. 'Easily distracted' and 'lacks concentration' were recurring comments on her end-of-year report, with exam results in most subjects not achieving the predicted grades. At the same time she was beginning to be unhappy at school, with friendship issues increasingly a problem. At home we attributed this to adolescence and offered advice and support whenever possible. However, the problems continued. Jesse seemed to be struggling with the amount of work set, and I began regular communications with her form tutor as we were both concerned about her evident unhappiness. The school nurse became involved as she was worried about Jesse frequently presenting with bruises and scratches. Following a fall at home where she banged her head and got a black eye, I was called in to see the Head. Although I was able to account for her injuries, I could not explain why they were so frequent – Jesse had always been 'accident-prone', with numerous wrist and ankle injuries over the years. As the school were so concerned they suggested Jesse should see the school counsellor. It was pure luck that the counsellor was Helen, who was familiar with dyspraxia and recognised Jesse's symptoms immediately.

I have worked in various schools; we have family members who are teachers, social workers and nurses, and specialists in learning difficulties. We all missed the signs of her disorder, simply accepting that Jesse was 'just Jesse' – rather chaotic, certainly unique but perfect just the way she was. The label doesn't change that, but it has changed the way we approach tasks in order for Jesse to manage them effectively.

Jesse's account

I started seeing Helen after the school became suspicious of my clumsy behaviour. I was often coming into school with cuts and bruises, and although I still do, the school have accepted dyspraxia as the cause. Having a name for what I am does change how I feel; it makes me feel less alone. I had been struggling but had always seen it as a fault in myself – not being good enough or trying hard enough, although I knew I was trying harder than others seemed to be.

Helen's account

Jesse was referred to me for emotional reasons in my role as a school counsellor – but I always try to unpick all possible factors that might be contributing to a child's unhappiness. Once I got round to asking Jesse and her mother a few questions about Jesse's early development, I started to suspect dyspraxia and suggested that I do a formal assessment.

Jesse herself completed our Dyspraxia Questionnaire for ages 12–14. She checked herself as 'definitely' having problems with: a messy room; using maths equipment; interpreting and drawing maps in geography; and writing legibly. She answered 'somewhat' to having problems with: organising school files; drawing in science; doing DT; finishing examinations and written work within the given time; and a sense of direction. She checked 'no problems' for organising and presenting written work.

The assessment showed Jesse to be a verbally bright girl, in the top 4 per cent of her age group with excellent expectations for her academic progress. Her visual-spatial skills were relatively poor, however, with some test scores quite a bit below her actual age level. The two tests of nonverbal processing speed were both very poor indeed and put her in the lowest 5 per cent (substantially below her age level). These showed she had the fine motor control and eye-hand co-ordination difficulties typical of many children with handwriting problems. Further testing revealed good reading accuracy, very good reading comprehension, acceptable spelling – but slow handwriting (largely in print to compensate for her problems with legibility), inefficient (slow) reading, and difficulties with written maths though not mathematical reasoning. Additional testing of underlying difficulties showed no problems with the 'dyslexia sensitive' tests (as expected, as she had no problems with literacy) but poor copy drawing and visual memory, and slow speed of processing on yet another type of task (letter and number naming).

The results of all the tests of underlying skills and capabilities showed a picture consistent with those of the educational tests. Jesse clearly had dyspraxia – or, the better description in her case, nonverbal learning difficulties – with visual-spatial skills, fine motor speed and speed of processing all problematic. Her history of clumsiness also suggested some gross motor problems.

All in all, the difficulties Jesse has would certainly be expected to make school life quite a challenge for her. She has managed very well over the years – to her considerable credit – but her difficulties have now started to catch up with her as the work and expectations from school have increased. But because Jesse is a bright girl and a hard worker with good verbal skills – and does not have dyslexia – it has been much trickier to spot her quite substantial underlying specific learning difficulty. And this has been despite having a mum who is very much on the ball!

Complete the General Questionnaire for your child's age group (either 7–11 or 12–14) to look at how well your child is progressing now with his or her nonverbal and writing skills.

Then think back to your child's early years to complete the Early Signs Questionnaire. At the end of each questionnaire look at the results to see whether or not there are signs that your child has dyspraxia. When you have all this information from the questionnaires, you can follow up any concerns using our Dyspraxia Checks for your child's age group.

GENERAL QUESTIONNAIRE: COULD YOUR CHILD HAVE DYSPRAXIA?

Ages 7–11
Does your child:

1. Have difficulty forming letters?
Yes, definitely ❑   Yes, somewhat ❑   No ❑

2. Have difficulty with joined-up writing?
Yes, definitely ❑   Yes, somewhat ❑   No ❑

3. Have difficulty writing legibly?
Yes, definitely ❑   Yes, somewhat ❑   No ❑

4. Show unwillingness to put pen to paper?
Yes, definitely ❑   Yes, somewhat ❑   No ❑

5. Have difficulty setting out written sums, and keeping in columns?
Yes, definitely ❑   Yes, somewhat ❑   No ❑

6. Frequently knock things over/bang into things/fall over/break things?
Yes, definitely ❑   Yes, somewhat ❑   No ❑

7. Have difficulty in tying shoelaces or fastening clothes?
Yes, definitely ❑   Yes, somewhat ❑   No ❑

8. Have difficulty with bat and ball games, throwing and catching?
Yes, definitely ❑   Yes, somewhat ❑   No ❑

9. Have difficulty learning to ride a bike?
Yes, definitely ❑   Yes, somewhat ❑   No ❑

10. Have difficulty using a knife and fork properly?
Yes, definitely ❑   Yes, somewhat ❑   No ❑

11. Have difficulty following directions/knowing left and right and back and front/following sequences of instructions?
Yes, definitely ❑   Yes, somewhat ❑   No ❑

Ages 12–14
Does he/she:

1. Still have problems with writing legibly?
Yes, definitely ❑   Yes, somewhat ❑   No ❑

2. Have trouble using maths equipment (ruler/compass/protractor)?
Yes, definitely ❑   Yes, somewhat ❑   No ❑

3. Have difficulty interpreting and drawing maps in geography?
Yes, definitely ❑   Yes, somewhat ❑   No ❑

4. Find it hard to understand and 'read' graphs and charts?
Yes, definitely ❑   Yes, somewhat ❑   No ❑

5. Have difficulty drawing diagrams in science?
Yes, definitely ❑   Yes, somewhat ❑   No ❑

6. Have trouble with layout in written maths?
Yes, definitely ❑   Yes, somewhat ❑   No ❑

7. Have difficulties with practical subjects such as DT or electronics?
Yes, definitely ❑   Yes, somewhat ❑   No ❑

8. Fail to finish exams or written work in the time given?
Yes, definitely ❑   Yes, somewhat ❑   No ❑

9. Have difficulty organising and presenting written work – such as making paragraphs, using full stops and other punctuation appropriately?
Yes, definitely ❑   Yes, somewhat ❑   No ❑

10. Have problems organising school files and papers?
Yes, definitely ❑   Yes, somewhat ❑   No ❑

11. Have a messy and untidy room and desk?
Yes, definitely ❑   Yes, somewhat ❑   No ❑

12. Have a poor sense of direction and get lost easily?
Yes, definitely ❑   Yes, somewhat ❑   No ❑

Results: General Questionnaire

As before, if you ticked the 'Yes, definitely' box for most of the questions – or even many of the 'Yes, somewhat' boxes – you would be right in thinking your child could have dyspraxia. If so, it would be worth following up with the checks on page 50.

If you ticked mostly 'No', it is unlikely that your child has dyspraxia.

EARLY SIGNS QUESTIONNAIRE (FOR ALL AGE GROUPS)

As a pre-schooler, did your child:

1. Stand and walk late (as a rough guide most children are standing unaided by 12 months and walking by 18 months)?
Yes, definitely ❑   Yes, somewhat ❑   No ❑

2. Bump into things and fall over a lot?
Yes, definitely ❑   Yes, somewhat ❑   No ❑

3. Have difficulty standing on one leg?
Yes, definitely ❑   Yes, somewhat ❑   No ❑

4. Have difficulty learning to get dressed?
Yes, definitely ❑   Yes, somewhat ❑   No ❑

5. Eat messily and spill food?
Yes, definitely ❑   Yes, somewhat ❑   No ❑

6. Have difficulty with puzzles such as inset boards and simple jigsaws, and have problems building a tower with blocks?
Yes, definitely ❑   Yes, somewhat ❑   No ❑

7. Have difficulty holding a pen and paintbrush – and have problems with drawing and copying simple shapes, houses or people?
Yes, definitely ❑   Yes, somewhat ❑   No ❑

8. And finally, is there a family history of clumsiness, disorganisation and/or poor handwriting?
Yes, definitely ❑   Yes, somewhat (distant members) ❑
No ❑

Results: Early Signs Questionnaire

If you ticked 'Yes, definitely' for most of the questions, then you have good reason to be concerned that your child might have dyspraxia. Consider the results of the General Questionnaire too and follow up with the checks to find out more (see below).

If you ticked 'Yes, somewhat' for many items, your child may be at risk for dyspraxia. Use the results of the General Questionnaire and the checks (below) to help you decide whether or not there is indeed a problem.

If you ticked 'No' for most of the items, then it is unlikely that your child has dyspraxia.

YOUR OWN CHECKS

Try out the five checks below. Use pencil and paper where necessary (or do it on the book page). Do not provide a rubber/eraser. Do each only once as you want to see how your child manages 'cold', without an opportunity to practise.

Checks for ages 7–11

Co-ordination and balance

Ask your child to do these things one after the other:

1. Close your eyes and touch your nose with your pointing (index) finger.
2. Now stand on one leg for as long as you can.
3. And now walk in a straight line putting one foot in front of the other with heel and toes touching.

For the next ones you will need a ball. Say to your child:

1. Catch this ball and throw it back (gently!)
2. Now throw the ball up in the air and clap your hands once before you catch it.
3. And now push the ball on the floor all around the chair with your hand(s).

Was your child able to do these things?

All easily ❑   Some with difficulty ❑   All with difficulty ❑

Mazes

Tell your child that he/she will now draw his/her way out of a maze. Show him/her the example below and explain how to do it. Tell him/her to start at the **Start arrow** and trace over the path to the **Finish arrow**.

Example maze

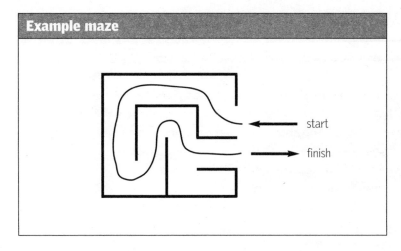

Now show your child the bigger maze. Tell him/her to keep the pencil on the paper the whole time and stay inside the path lines. Tell him/her not to go up a blind alley (that is scored as an error) or to go through or touch a wall (also an error). He/she has to find the right way out (going all the way out) to finish. If your child does go into a blind alley, tell him/her to backtrack and keep going to find the way out. Score for errors at the end.

Maze

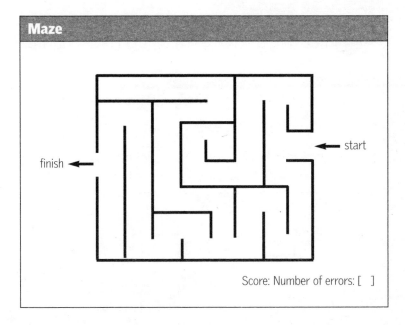

Score: Number of errors: [ ]

How did your child do? Children of 7–11 should be able to do this quickly, staying within the lines and making no errors (or only one or two errors for a 7 year old).

Copying a passage
Show your child the story overleaf while you read it out loud. Then ask him/her to copy it on some lined paper (school exercise books are best). Eight to 11 year olds should be asked to copy all of the story, but 7 year olds may need to be told to do just as much as they can.

Story – Jack's Fairground Ride

It was Jack's first roller coaster ride. The rails went almost up to the sky, and he had seen people screaming as they plunged down. But when they got out, he could see them laughing. Now he was in a car himself. Jack's little sister sat next to him. Mum and Dad were on the ground, waving. He wished they were coming on the roller coaster. Clang! The cars started off with a bump. Up, up, up. Oh no! Jack felt sick. He held his sister's hand. She was smiling. Why wasn't she scared?

Now, how did your child do?

a. Is it difficult to read what he/she has written?
Yes, definitely ❏   Yes, somewhat ❏   No ❏

b. Is he/she unable to keep the letters within or on the line?
Yes, definitely ❏   Yes, somewhat ❏   No ❏

c. Would you describe his/her writing (bearing in mind what you would expect for his/her age) as untidy and messy?
Yes, definitely ❑   Yes, somewhat ❑   No ❑

d. Did he/she find the writing a struggle and take a long time to do it?
Yes, definitely ❑   Yes, somewhat ❑   No ❑

If you ticked 'Yes, definitely' for most of these, your child clearly has writing problems.

Symmetry

Ask your child to look at the pictures below. Then ask him/her to draw the mirror image on the other side of the line (as in the example below) so that both sides look exactly the same.

Example (ask your child to trace over the dotted line)

Now ask your child to try this one for him/herself

Now look at how your child managed.

a. Did he/she have difficulty in copying exactly?
Yes, definitely ❑   Yes, somewhat ❑   No ❑

b. If he/she had difficulty with it, was he/she aware of it? (Ask if he/she thinks it is a good copy.)
Yes, definitely ❑   Yes, somewhat ❑   No ❑

Children of 7–11 should be able to make a reasonable mirror drawing. If your child had difficulty – and especially if he/she was not aware that the copy was poor – these are signs of dyspraxia.

Drawing shapes

Give your child the instruction: 'Draw a diamond *inside a square*. Make the points of the diamond touch the sides of the square at the centre point of each line. Do it as carefully as you can.' You can repeat the instruction once if needed – but don't repeat it after he/she has started drawing.

It should look reasonably close to this (see below, but *do not show this drawing to your child*):

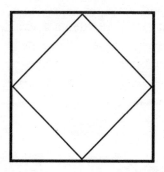

Next say to your child: 'Now draw a figure with six equal sides, a hexagon, *inside a circle* – with the points of the hexagon touching the circle.'

It should look like this (again, keep this drawing to yourself):

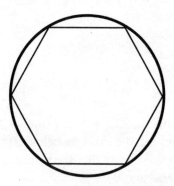

Look at how your child managed.

a. Did he/she have difficulty producing the *individual shapes* correctly with the right number of lines (taken from both drawings)? See below for how each individual shape should look:

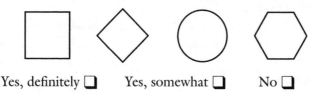

Yes, definitely ❑   Yes, somewhat ❑   No ❑

Children of 7–11 should be able to manage these reasonably well, though the youngest ones might have trouble with the hexagon.

b. Did your child have difficulty drawing the two shapes in the correct *relationship* to each other – with the diamond properly *inside* the square and the points *touching* the sides of the square, and the hexagon *inside* the circle, however poorly it is drawn?
Yes, definitely ❑   Yes, somewhat ❑   No ❑

Children of 9–11 should be able to draw the individual shapes accurately *and* make a reasonable attempt at putting one shape inside another. However, children of 7–8 could still be expected to find this quite hard.

Checks for ages 12–14

Now for the checks for the teenage years. Of course, you need to explain to your child why you are doing this. By this stage, hopefully, you and your child will have talked about any problems with school work. These checks to find out more about the difficulties your child is having should be explained as being useful for finding ways to help.

Mazes

Tell your child that he/she will now draw his/her way out of a maze. Show him/her the example below and explain how to do it. Tell him/her to start at the **Start arrow** and trace over the path to the **Finish arrow**.

Example maze

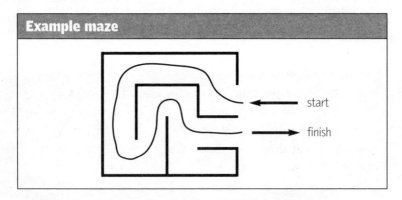

Now show your child the bigger maze. Tell him/her to keep the pencil on the paper the whole time, stay inside the path lines and work quickly. Tell him/her not to go up a blind alley (scored as an error) or to go through or touch a wall (also an error). He/she has to find the right way out (going all the way out) to finish. If your child does go into a blind alley, tell him/her to backtrack and keep going to find the way out. Score for errors at the end.

Maze

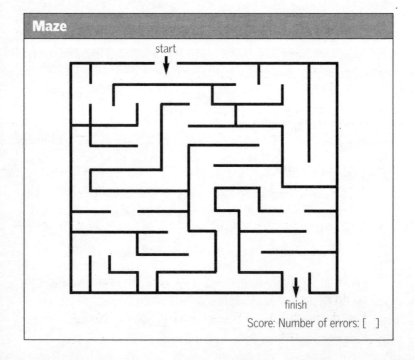

Score: Number of errors: [ ]

Children of 12–14 should be able to do this quickly, staying within the lines and making no more than one error.

Writing to dictation

Read the following passage out loud (without showing it) to your child. Then ask him/her to write it down on some lined paper (school exercise books are best) while you reread it slowly. You can repeat the words if necessary – it is not meant to be a test of memory.

Story – Go-karting

Red and white barriers have turned the supermarket car park into a go-kart race track. Six cars painted with flashy logos twist and turn around the narrow circuit. Boys and girls like astronauts in shiny suits and helmets whip their steering wheels left, right, left again. A roar fills the air with crashing, buzzing thunder. Tyres scream as in pain. Who will win? Who will grow up to be a Formula One champion?

Now, how did your child do?

a. Was it difficult to read his/her writing?
    Yes, definitely ❑   Yes, somewhat ❑   No ❑

b. Was he/she unable to keep the letters within or on the line?
    Yes, definitely ❑   Yes, somewhat ❑   No ❑

c. Would you describe the handwriting as untidy and messy?
    Yes, definitely ❑   Yes, somewhat ❑   No ❑

d. Did he/she find the writing a struggle and take a long time to do it?
    Yes, definitely ❑   Yes, somewhat ❑   No ❑

If you answered 'Yes, definitely' to most of these, your child clearly has handwriting difficulties.

Symmetry
Ask your teenager to look at the diagrams below. Then ask him/her to draw the mirror image on the other side of the line (as in the example below) so that both sides look exactly the same.

Example of how to do it – trace over the dotted line

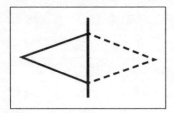

Finish the drawing so that it matches the side already drawn

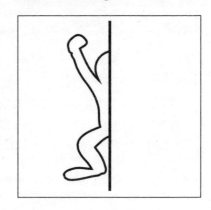

And here's another to do

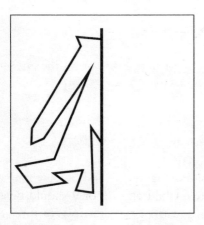

Now look at how he/she managed.

a. Did he/she have difficulty in producing a close copy in each case?

Yes, definitely ❑   Yes, somewhat ❑   No ❑

b. If he/she had difficulty in making accurate copies, was he/she aware of it? (Ask if he/she thought the copies were good to help you answer this.)

Yes, definitely ❑   Yes, somewhat ❑   No ❑

Children of 12–14 should be able to make an accurate mirror drawing. If your child had difficulty – and especially if he/she was not aware that the copy was poor – these are signs of dyspraxia.

Drawing shapes

Ask your teenager to draw some three-dimensional shapes. 'Draw a cylinder and a cone, touching at the top but not overlapping, at right angles to each other. The point of the cone should touch the top of the cylinder.' (You can repeat the instruction once if needed – but only before he/she starts drawing.)

It should look like this (remember to keep this correct version to yourself):

Next say: 'Draw a cube with a diamond on each individual face. Each point of the diamond should touch the sides of the cube.'

It should look like this (but again keep the correct version to yourself):

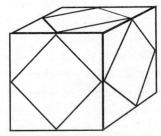

Now assess the results.

a. Did he/she have difficulty in producing the correct shapes?
Yes, definitely ❏   Yes, somewhat ❏   No ❏

b. Did he/she have difficulty with the relationships between the shapes?
Yes, definitely ❏   Yes, somewhat ❏   No ❏

Children of 12–14 should be able to draw even three-dimensional shapes reasonably accurately.

Results: Checks for ages 7–11 and 12–14

You have now completed the checks for your child. How did it all go? Were there lots of errors? Were there struggles to put pen to paper? Did each item take a long time to do? Did you see signs of frustration? Were the results messy and untidy?

If your answer is 'Yes' to most of these questions, this is a good indication of dyspraxia or nonverbal learning difficulty.

If the results of the questionnaires and checks point to your child having dyspraxia, you need to take action and talk to teachers about what can be done to help.

THE WAY FORWARD

Act immediately

The one approach to dyspraxia that is *not* helpful to children is to 'do nothing' and 'wait and see'. It is a common myth that parents should not worry about children having dyspraxia/DCD because 'they will outgrow it'. Studies have shown that for most children with dyspraxia this is not the case. The difficulties persist at least until early adolescence and in many instances for much longer. This is why dyspraxia needs to be treated seriously, with action being taken as early as possible. Having said that, many verbally able children with dyspraxia are able to manage – or be helped to manage – by using their good language skills to compensate for their difficulties.

No simple treatments – but don't despair

Dyspraxia covers such a wide range of difficulties (and knock-on effects). Therefore it is not surprising that it has proved very hard to find treatments that make a difference. Perhaps the best approach is to work on the visible effects of the dyspraxia by, for example:

■ Working to improve letter formation, neatness/presentation and writing speed – through direct teaching.

■ Supplying helpful materials such as special pen grips and angled paper supports.

■ Encouraging use of computers for written work and supplying typewritten class notes.

■ Making accommodations within the school environment by giving time extensions for homework and projects, and extra time for written tests and exams.

Best of all is to combine these practical suggestions with a 'cognitive approach' that teaches children to talk their way around their problems and through solutions – for instance, using a series of verbal instructions to work through a street map (which the child with dyspraxia would find visually confusing). Another example is making a written plan before starting an essay. What is important is to make these practical and cognitive approaches part of everyday life – what Professor of Education David Sugden calls 'ecological intervention'. This is done by drawing on the child's strengths to tackle the particular task being learned and by making it relevant for the situation.

A number of physical therapies have been developed that aim to treat the underlying perceptual and motor difficulties shown by children with dyspraxia. One of the most popular is **sensory integration therapy**. This uses a series of sensory exercises to improve how the child 'integrates' or puts together information from the different senses (touch, motor, visual, body posture and hearing). Unfortunately, there is no convincing evidence to show that this type of therapy on its own makes any difference to children's school performance or day-to-day life skills – other than possibly improving self-esteem or motivation because the problem is being recognised and addressed in a positive and supportive way. Nor is there any known effective drug treatment for dyspraxia. However, children with DAMP (see page 40) who have attention and hyperactivity problems may benefit from medication that specifically targets their attention difficulties (see Chapter 4 for more details.)

■ ■ ■

Dyspraxia is a common specific learning difficulty, like dyslexia, but is harder to pick up, not least because people are less on the lookout for it. Individual children may be different in the exact problems they show, but all will have problems with either motor or perceptual skills – and often both. Having dyspraxia can lower children's self-esteem as well as affect their classroom performance. There is no clear underlying cause, but genes play a part. Teachers and parents need to focus on the child's individual difficulties from an early stage, without waiting to see if the problems are outgrown.

If the results of your own checks and the questionnaires point to a difficulty, it would be a good idea to talk to your child's teacher. Together you can consider a plan of action for school (Chapter 7) and home (Chapters 10 and 11).

3

Could Your Child Have Specific Language Impairment (SLI)?

Children with specific language impairment have difficulty in understanding and using spoken language. Speech impediments such as stammering are not included here – only problems of language and communication. Having a speech and language learning difficulty means that the child's **understanding** and **use** of *spoken* language are not up to the level of their nonverbal (visual and practical) skills. Most children with language difficulties – however severe – will still try hard to *communicate* with others. They may use their eyes, finger pointing (and other gestures) and sounds instead of words to make their needs known. These children do not have as their main difficulty a problem with hearing; nor do they have psychiatric problems that would explain their poor language. The term used by professionals to describe such difficulties is **specific language impairment** (**SLI**). SLI is a specific learning difficulty, since these children do not have problems in all areas of learning.

SLI QUIZ

Read each statement and circle TRUE or FALSE, then look at the following pages for the answers and more information.

1. Speech and language difficulties show a very different pattern from child to child.   TRUE or FALSE

2. Children with speech and language difficulties are very often autistic. TRUE or FALSE

3. Speech and language difficulties affect fewer than 2 per cent of children. TRUE or FALSE

4. Girls are just as likely as boys to have speech or language problems. TRUE or FALSE

5. Language difficulties are caused by parents not talking enough to their young children. TRUE or FALSE

6. Brain damage at birth is the most frequent cause of speech and language problems. TRUE or FALSE

7. Many children with early speech and language problems are likely also to have reading difficulties later on.

TRUE or FALSE

8. Many children who have been late to talk will have caught up by the time they start school. TRUE or FALSE

9. Parents have a bigger role than professionals in helping their child overcome language problems. TRUE or FALSE

Now how did you do?

1. Speech and language difficulties show a very different pattern from child to child. TRUE

2. Children with speech and language difficulties are very often autistic. FALSE

3. Speech and language difficulties affect fewer than 2 per cent of children. FALSE

4. Girls are just as likely as boys to have speech or language problems. FALSE

5. Language difficulties are caused by parents not talking enough to their young children. FALSE

6. Brain damage at birth is the most frequent cause of speech and language problems. FALSE

7. Many children with early speech and language problems are likely also to have reading difficulties later on. TRUE

8. Many children who have been late to talk will have caught up by the time they start school. TRUE

9. Parents have a bigger role than professionals in helping their child overcome language problems. TRUE

If you got 7 or more correct then you have a good understanding of language difficulties. If you got fewer than 7 correct, it may reflect the fact that language difficulties are not as often talked about in the press as dyslexia and dyspraxia. In this chapter we will show you how important language is for classroom learning.

FACTS ABOUT SLI

SLI is fairly common

SLI has been shown to affect large numbers of children, although it is not quite as common as dyslexia. Around 6 per cent of pre-schoolers have SLI, but around half of these will have largely caught up by the time they are five. Only 3 per cent of children have SLI that persists into their school years. More boys than girls are affected, as with dyslexia and dyspraxia.

SLI is inherited

It is important to explode the myth that SLI is caused by parents not talking enough to their young children. As Professor Steven Pinker, an authority on how language develops, has said: 'In general, language acquisition is a stubbornly robust process; from what we can tell, there is virtually no way to prevent it from happening short of raising a child in a barrel.' Language is built into our genes, so children need to hear very little speech for their language systems to get started. (Some hearing of speech is needed, as shown by the language problems of the profoundly deaf.) It therefore follows that SLI has a genetic basis. While SLI is rarely caused by brain damage, neurological studies have shown that children with language difficulties do have subtle abnormalities in the left (language) side of their brains. This demonstrates a biological rather than environmental cause.

Difficulties show a different pattern from child to child

Children with SLI typically show a history of being late to start talking, and their language continues to develop slowly. However, they can show hugely different patterns of strengths and weaknesses. They are, in fact, a very mixed group, and the pattern of difficulties for one child can itself change over time. It is not so much that there are different categories or subtypes of SLI; it is rather the case that research has so far failed to show separate SLI groups. However, many professionals assessing and teaching children with SLI find it useful to group them according to the kind of language difficulty they show:

Receptive and expressive language difficulties

Children can be grouped according to whether they have **receptive** or **expressive** language difficulties. Receptive language refers to children's *understanding* of what is said to them. Expressive language refers to children's ability to speak to, and to communicate with, others. Children with either receptive or expressive difficulties will have a **limited vocabulary**, and will usually find it **hard to put words together** to form a complete sentence. Receptive language problems generally cause the greatest difficulties for the child. Children with receptive difficulties that carry on beyond the pre-school years are likely to have long-term and severe communication difficulties and classroom learning problems – and they will almost certainly have expressive language difficulties too. However, children with expressive language difficulties who have relatively good receptive (understanding) skills are likely to have fewer communication problems. Determining whether a child has a receptive or expressive difficulty (or both) is important for knowing what sort of help should be given. But children with language difficulties of any sort ought to receive help from a speech and language therapist in the pre-school years.

Phonological problems

Children can also be grouped according to whether they have difficulties in producing speech sounds accurately – **phonological problems**. This affects their *articulation* (how clearly they speak and so how understandable they are to other people). Speech therapy is important for children whose phonological problems persist beyond the age of three in order to make their speech clear for all to understand. Children who start school with persistent speech difficulties are also at high risk of literacy problems.

Social communication

Finally, children can be grouped according to their ability to use language for **social communication**. Children who have a social communication difficulty (or pragmatic disorder) find it hard to take turns in conversation, or to understand complex social cues and implied (rather than clearly stated) information. This means that jokes, irony and proverbs are usually lost on them – and they are likely to interpret them literally (so 'green-fingered' would mean someone whose fingers are green rather than a good gardener). Children on the autistic spectrum typically have a pragmatic language disorder. However, not all children who struggle with pragmatic aspects of language have autism – only those who also display the complex behavioural and obsessive difficulties typical of autism. Children with an autistic spectrum disorder are likely to use language in even more atypical (or deviant) ways than children with a pragmatic disorder. For example, they may reverse pronouns, referring to themselves as 'you' when they mean 'I', or they may repeat the same phrases over and over again without communicating anything meaningful.

SLI can affect nonverbal ability

Although children with SLI are defined as having more problems with speech and language than with nonverbal intelligence, in practice the relationship between verbal and nonverbal skills is rather more complicated. Some children with severe speech and language problems are likely to have, or to develop over time, nonverbal learning difficulties. This is because language may be needed for the processing of complex nonverbal tasks. Children might not be able to 'talk their way through' a nonverbal task because they lack the vocabulary that directs their thinking – for example, finding a route using a map. There may even be a knock-on effect in that the children's nonverbal IQ scores may go down over time.

Language difficulties affect learning in the classroom

The most immediate effect of SLI is on how well the child understands and can follow what the teacher says – especially if the teacher talks very quickly. Additionally, short-term verbal memory difficulties are often seen in children with SLI. This means that they find it hard to remember what has just been said to them. Children who do not understand or remember what others say will find it hard to *concentrate* in lessons, and so might be seen as having **attention** problems. Teachers need to make extra time for children with SLI – to make sure that the children's views and opinions are voiced and heard, that they ask for help when they need it, and that they have understood the content of the lesson. Children who find it hard to follow lessons and to communicate soon fall behind in their learning.

SLI and literacy

Many children with early speech and language problems have difficulties with **reading and writing** too. There are differences in how SLI affects literacy, depending on the particular type of speech and language difficulty the child shows.

Children with poor speech are at high risk for difficulties in spelling (and possibly reading). However, if the problem is a fairly mild one, like a lisp, then progress is usually fine. Children with receptive language problems (who also have limited vocabularies and poor understanding of grammar) will certainly have difficulty understanding what they read, even if they can read the words accurately. Eight to 10 per cent of all children are able to read words but cannot understand what they read. These 'poor reading comprehenders' almost always have language problems. Such children usually go unnoticed within the classroom because of their good reading accuracy. It is important not to assume that teaching children to decode, so improving their reading accuracy, will also lead to improvements in reading comprehension. As reading comprehension problems tend to persist well beyond the primary school years, it is helpful if children have been identified as 'at risk' as young as possible so their language difficulties can be treated early – this will reduce the chance of them becoming poor reading comprehenders.

Children with expressive language difficulties who have problems in saying what they think and feel can't write it down either.

SLI and other aspects of school life

The classroom learning problems of children with SLI will in turn affect *all* their academic subjects. Children with language difficulties are very likely also to have problems with maths. Their poor short-term verbal memory affects their ability to do simple sums, to learn number facts and to count accurately.

The effect of speech and language difficulties extends beyond the classroom to children's **social life** too. Difficulty in communicating affects the ability to make (and keep) friends. Children with language difficulties may also become very unhappy, withdrawn and isolated.

Did your child have speech and language difficulties during his/her early years? Sometimes these difficulties persist into the school years, even though they may not be as obvious as they once were. Fill in the questionnaires below. The General Questionnaire looks at your child's language today. Then think back to your child's early years to complete the Early Signs Questionnaire.

GENERAL QUESTIONNAIRE:
COULD YOUR CHILD HAVE SLI?

1. Does he/she have difficulty following verbal instructions (especially if there are several parts to your instructions – usually failing to do at least one of them)?
Yes, definitely ❏   Yes, somewhat ❏   No ❏

2. Does he/she have difficulty following 'narrative', that is, following a story such as in a film or on television, or when you describe something that has happened?
Yes, definitely ❏   Yes, somewhat ❏   No ❏

3. Does he/she have problems pronouncing long words accurately?
Yes, definitely ❏   Yes, somewhat ❏   No ❏

4. Does he/she frequently have 'word-finding' difficulties – that is, knows what he/she wants to say but just can't find the right word?
Yes, definitely ❏   Yes, somewhat ❏   No ❏

5. Does he/she still make a lot of grammatical errors when talking?
Yes, definitely ❏   Yes, somewhat ❏   No ❏

6. When he/she tries to explain something to others, do the words come out jumbled, making it hard for others to follow?
Yes, definitely ❏   Yes, somewhat ❏   No ❏

7. When talking to people does he/she get fixed on one topic or find it hard to understand jokes?
Yes, definitely ❏   Yes, somewhat ❏   No ❏

EARLY SIGNS QUESTIONNAIRE

Think back to your child's *pre-school* years.

1. Was he/she late to talk? (Usually first words appear by 12 months, short two- to three-word phrases by 15–18 months, short but complete sentences by 2½ years.)
Yes, definitely ❑   Yes, somewhat ❑   No ❑

2. Was his/her speech unclear and difficult for others to understand?
Yes, definitely ❑   Yes, somewhat ❑   No ❑

3. Was a speech and language therapist ever recommended?
Yes ❑   No ❑

4. Did he/she have difficulty talking to other children during play?
Yes, definitely ❑   Yes, somewhat ❑   No ❑

5. Did he/she have difficulty playing with small toys (miniature people or animals, tea or train sets, and so on) for pretend/imaginative games?
Yes, definitely ❑   Yes, somewhat ❑   No ❑

Results: General and Early Signs Questionnaires

If you have answered 'Yes, definitely' (or 'Yes' for question 3 in the Early Signs Questionnaire) – and even 'Yes, somewhat' – for most of the questions in both the General and Early Signs Questionnaires, then your child had early speech and language difficulties that are continuing into the school years. These difficulties are likely to affect him or her in the classroom in various ways. If you answered 'No' to most of the questions, then your child's language seems to be fine.

YOUR OWN CHECKS

Checks for ages 7-11

Repeating nonsense words

Ask your child to repeat the following nonsense words back to you (look back at the guide to pronunciation on page 26 and practise if you need to). These same nonsense words appeared in Chapter 1; if you already carried out that check, then just note the score again here. You might find it helpful to tick each syllable said correctly as your child says it. Say each nonsense word only once. Both the pronunciation of each syllable and the order have to be right to score as correct.

moofip	[mōō – fĭp]
chezmong	[chĕz – mŏng]
plashleeguv	[plăsh – lēē – gŭv]
tuvzigop	[tŭv – zĭ –gŏp]
thipundojee	[thĭp – ŭn – dō – jēē]
shavroozepgos	[shăv – rōō – zĕp – gŏs]

[/6] correct

Repeating sentences

Ask your child to repeat these sentences back to you exactly as you said them. Ask him/her to **look at you** and **listen carefully** before you say them – and say each sentence only once. Put a line through each word your child gets wrong, and make a note of the number of errors made in each sentence. An error could be:

- leaving out a word
- saying a different word
- getting any words in the wrong order

	Number of Errors

1. The boy stood in front of the class. _____

2. My ginger cat drank his milk and fell asleep. _____

3. Six girls raced along the bumpy road. _____

4. Dad is going to buy pizza and ice cream for dinner. _____

5. Next week, when our computer is mended, we can all go on the internet. _____

6. Put away your books and pencils in your trays before you line up for lunch. _____

Total Errors _____

Understanding rules of grammar

Ask your child to **say out loud what the end of the sentence should be** after you say the first part. Point to the pictures in the box below as you say each sentence (answers given overleaf).

1. Susie saw one star in the sky but James saw two _____

2. Here is one mouse and here are two _____

3. Jack likes to climb. Here is a ladder he has _____

4. The pirate steals the jewels. Here are the jewels he has

_____

5. Zack likes to write. This is what he _____

6. Lee keeps pets. Here is a puppy Lee has _____

Answers
1. *Stars*
2. *Mice*
3. *Climbed*
4. *Stolen*
5. *Wrote*
6. *Kept*

Checks for ages 12–14
Repeating nonsense words

Ask your teenager to repeat the following nonsense words back to you. It might be a good idea to practise saying them yourself first (see the pronunciation guide on page 26). Tick each syllable he/she gets right as you go along. Say each nonsense word only once. Both the pronunciation of each syllable and the order have to be right to score as correct.

plashleeguv	[plăsh – lēē – gŭv]
tuvzigop	[tŭv – zĭ –gŏp]
thipundojee	[thĭp – ŭn – dō – jēē]
shavroozepgos	[shăv – rōō – zĕp – gŏs]
febchagzaylinwoo	[fĕb-chăg-zāy-lĭn-wōō]
slockfeeblatrookep	[slŏck-fēē-blăt-rōō-kĕp]

[/6] correct

Repeating sentences

Ask your teenager to repeat these sentences back to you exactly as you say them. Ask him/her to **look at you** and **listen carefully** before you say them – and say each sentence only once. Put a line through each word your child gets wrong, and make a note of the number of errors made in each sentence. An error could be:

- leaving out a word
- saying a different word
- getting any words in the wrong order

Number
of Errors

1. After I finished my homework, I watched
television for an hour.   _____

2. In the park, the gardener raked, mowed and
watered the grass.   _____

3. The pupils in the science class did an experiment
making blue crystals in a test tube.   _____

4. The boy bought trainers for £15, but he was
cross when they fell apart after two weeks.   _____

5. Three girls were sitting at a table in the library
working on a geography project.   _____

6. Did you remember to take your maths book,
your lunch box and your sports kit out of
your locker?   _____

Total Errors   _____

Results: Checks for ages 7–11 and 12–14

For both age groups, if your child made only a few errors on
both repeating nonsense words and repeating sentences, then he
or she is not showing obvious signs of having an underlying
language difficulty. For the additional test of understanding rules
of grammar for the 7–11 year olds only, no errors would be
expected.

On the other hand, if he or she found these checks quite hard
and made a number of errors, then there may be a persisting
underlying language difficulty. If, after looking back at the questionnaire answers and the results of the checks together, you feel
there is *any* reason to be concerned, then do talk this through
with the teachers.

THE WAY FORWARD

Supporting the child with SLI in school

Because language difficulties have such a marked and far-reaching effect on children's progress and happiness at school, it is really important to give them a lot of support including:

- making sure that everyone talks to the child slowly and in short sentences
- checking that the child has understood what has been said, repeating and rephrasing sentences as needed
- providing strategies for concentrating and staying on task – for instance, giving smaller amounts of work at a time, setting easier short-term goals and praising each success
- providing additional and specialist support teaching for reading, spelling and maths from an early stage
- providing emotional support by 'tutor mentoring' (that is, giving the child time to talk alone with a teacher about any difficulties or worries) and perhaps a 'buddy system' where an older child looks out for the child when needed
- helping the other children in the class to understand the difficulties of a child with SLI and offering them some practical suggestions for giving friendly support

What happens later to children with SLI?

Some children's language problems appear to resolve completely by early to middle childhood. Professor Dorothy Bishop, a psychologist specialising in children's language, has described these children as 'late bloomers' – they go on to make good use of language and they have no special academic difficulties. The problem is thought to be that the brain is slow to mature. There is another group of children who seem to overcome their early speech delay but continue to have subtle language problems such as 'word-finding difficulties' (finding the right word to use); they may pepper their speech with 'ums', 'ers' and 'whatevers' or just get stuck and come to a halt. These children are at risk of reading (accuracy and comprehension) and spelling problems. A third group have severe language difficulties that persist. There is a *huge* variation in how children with speech and language difficulties *manage* during their school years. What actually happens to any one child depends on:

- How severe the language problem is – in general, the milder the problem in the first place the better the outcome (those with receptive language difficulties are likely to face the most problems later on).
- Whether the child's language problems lead to attention and/or social difficulties that could then create a risk for later psychological troubles.
- The level of the child's practical and visual-spatial skills, as shown by their nonverbal IQ; good nonverbal skills appear to protect children from some of the worst effects of their language problems.
- How early the child's language difficulties are recognised and how quickly action is taken.
- Whether or not there is *active involvement* of parents from an early age to help their child manage and get around their language (and educational and social) difficulties; daily help from parents makes an even bigger difference than anything professionals can provide.

■　■　■

SLI is a specific learning difficulty, like dyslexia and dyspraxia, because one set of skills (spoken language) is less well developed than another (visual and perceptual abilities). SLI is a common problem and can have widespread and long-standing effects on children's education and even their friendships. Early language difficulties put children at risk for dyslexia.

If the results of your questionnaires and checks point to a language difficulty, discuss with your child's teacher how the difficulties affect learning and what can be done to help.

4

Could Your Child Have Attention Deficit with Hyperactivity Disorder (ADHD)?

Does your child have difficulties in concentrating that are so much of a problem that they might amount to a behaviour disorder? ADHD (Attention Deficit with Hyperactivity Disorder) is not just a fancy label to excuse bad behaviour. Some parents may worry about the social stigma of the 'ADHD' label – maybe fearing that their child's difficult behaviour is not only an embarrassment but also somehow reflects badly on their parenting. This should not be the case. If you are a parent of a child with ADHD, you should not feel ashamed; the difficulties are neither your nor your child's fault. ADHD is a complex problem; 'bad behaviour' may often be a feature but the core difficulties are **poor attention (or inattention), lack of impulse control (impulsivity),** and **hyperactivity.**

Inattention largely refers to the inability to keep 'on task', becoming distracted, and being unable to complete work in the classroom. It also includes reluctance to engage with people and activities, a tendency to break off in the middle of tasks, lack of attention to detail and not listening. How well children can concentrate on non-academic activities can also be very telling – those with severe problems may not even be able to stick long at doing things they might be expected to enjoy.

Impulsivity describes behaviours where children can't stop themselves doing what they have the urge to do. They don't seem to have a 'self stop' button. They do things without thinking, even things they know to be wrong or stupid, but when asked why they did it they will say something along the lines of, 'Dunno, I just did!'

Hyperactivity is 'overactivity', with children running around a lot, never sitting still, fidgeting almost all the time and flitting from one thing to another – behaviour that is seen from a very early age. However, it is not the kind of overactivity expected in normally developing children – it's a significant notch up the intensity scale from this. It is a non-stop 'over the top' level of activity and it drives adults to distraction. It is also out of keeping with age (and often intelligence too).

Professor Eric Taylor, child neuropsychiatrist and authority on ADHD, has shown that 80 per cent of children with ADHD can be identified by two characteristic behaviours:

- Response inhibition – this means that they can't 'hold back' their actions when they need to, and so jump in quickly.
- Delay aversion – they can't wait for rewards but want them instantly, even if they could get a bigger reward by hanging on a bit longer.

In order to make a clear diagnosis of ADHD, the problems of attention, impulsivity and hyperactivity need to be shown at both home *and* school. If a child is fine at school but difficult at home, or difficult at school but fine at home, the problem is more likely to be due to emotional/behavioural causes than to ADHD. The attention difficulties should also be longstanding (lasting for at least six months) and not just a short-lived 'blip' in behaviour caused by some upset or worrying life event.

ADHD QUIZ

Try this quiz to see how much you already know about ADHD. Read each statement and circle TRUE or FALSE then look at the following pages for the answers and more information.

1. ADHD and ADD mean the same thing.   TRUE or FALSE

2. People with ADHD can be described as 'right-brain' thinkers.   TRUE or FALSE

3. Fewer girls than boys have ADHD.   TRUE or FALSE

4. ADHD is one of the most strongly inherited of all the specific learning disorders.   TRUE or FALSE

5. Most children with ADHD have trouble making and keeping friendships.   TRUE or FALSE

6. All children with ADHD fall behind educationally.

TRUE or FALSE

7. Medication is always the treatment of choice in ADHD.

TRUE or FALSE

8. Food additives can make ADHD worse for some children.

TRUE or FALSE

9. Most children completely outgrow their ADHD by the time they are seven.   TRUE or FALSE

are seven. FALSE

9. Most children completely outgrow their ADHD by the time they

8. Food additives can make ADHD worse for some children. TRUE

7. Medication is always the treatment of choice in ADHD. FALSE

6. All children with ADHD fall behind educationally. FALSE

friendships. TRUE

5. Most children with ADHD have trouble making and keeping

learning disorders. TRUE

4. ADHD is one of the most strongly inherited of all the specific

3. Fewer girls than boys have ADHD. TRUE

FALSE

2. People with ADHD can be described as 'right-brain' thinkers.

1. ADHD and ADD mean the same thing. FALSE

Now how did you do?

FACTS ABOUT ADHD

ADHD is common – but girls get missed

Three to 7 per cent of children in the UK are given a formal diagnosis of ADHD. Many more boys than girls – nine boys to every one girl – find their way into special clinics where they are diagnosed with ADHD. However, studies of children in the community show that three boys to one girl is the truer ratio. What these figures indicate is that attention difficulties in girls are often under-recognised; fewer girls with ADHD get to special clinics and therefore their ADHD is not picked up. This happens because girls are less likely than boys to be loud, noisy and markedly overactive. They may instead 'internalise' their attention problems by being anxious and withdrawn in their social relationships.

ADHD versus ADD

ADHD is a serious and far-reaching problem. Like all the other specific learning difficulties discussed so far, there is a continuum from mild to very severe. Many professionals like to separate ADD (Attention Deficit Disorder) from ADHD because some children have concentration problems but without the hyperactivity and high impulsivity elements. Some ADD children between the ages of four and six, boys in particular, have attentional skills that are developing more slowly than expected. Many of these *slow-maturing* children will improve in their concentration skills as they get older, especially if they have good teaching within well-structured classrooms. Many children with ADHD will show additional problems of antisocial behaviour in and out of school and will have problems in their relationships with others (adults and peers). ADD children are much less likely to have these kinds of difficulties. The separation of ADHD and ADD is useful because knowing the different patterns of difficulty affects which strategies are chosen to help the child.

ADHD and memory problems

It is important to recognise that some children who seem to have attention difficulties may in fact have a problem of 'working memory'. Professor Susan Gathercole at the Centre for Working Memory and Learning, University of York, describes working memory as a 'kind of mental jotting pad for storing information necessary for everyday activities such as remembering telephone numbers, following directions and instructions and keeping track of shopping list items while in the supermarket'. When memory becomes overloaded – too much for the child to cope with – vital information necessary to guide the ongoing activity is lost. The child forgets what he or she is doing or the instruction given and appears distracted. It is important to make sure that a child presenting with an attention problem does not in fact have an underlying problem with memory.

ADHD and the brain

The *cause* of ADHD has its roots in brain functioning, but it is not a 'right brain' or 'right brain versus left brain' issue. (The right brain is relevant for visual and creative learning, while the left brain is involved in language and reasoning.) ADHD is instead thought to be caused by a problem within the frontal lobe of the brain. The frontal lobes are directly behind the forehead and are involved in what is known as 'executive function' – that is, complex thinking, self-control and planning sequences of actions. Children with ADHD are sometimes described as having a 'dys-executive syndrome'.

ADHD is inherited – but environment is important too

Research has shown that ADHD is one of the most strongly inherited of all the specific learning difficulties. Children from families where there are several members with ADHD are *very much* at risk of having it too. Knowing where the problems are coming from helps parents to understand better why their child behaves the way he or she does – and will help pave the way for solutions.

That is not to say that environment is not important: it is. There are a number of ways in which a child's environment can affect ADHD:

- Low birth weight and birth complications can affect brain functioning (and so cause ADHD).

- Family stresses and strains can 'feed in' to make the problems worse (it is harder for parents to cope with a child's troublesome behaviour when they are trying to solve their own life crises).

- Children with ADHD are more likely to upset and annoy others by the irritating things they do and say. This has a knock-on effect on how people react and relate to them. Teachers in particular may become angry when a child distracts other children and disrupts the class – because they find it hard to control such children.

- Being able to make friends (and keep them) can be affected by having ADHD. Many children do not want to be associated with a child who is often in trouble, and they may even be frightened by the unpredictability and aggression of such a child. Youngsters with ADHD find themselves facing not only a barrage of criticism from teachers but also rejection by other children. This is very likely to make a child's behaviour even worse.

Teachers and parents need to be aware of how their (often perfectly reasonable) reactions to children's problematic behaviour can make things even harder for all concerned. Equally, if parents and teachers themselves change the way they relate to such children, this can in turn affect their behaviour for the better (see pages 90–1 for some strategies).

Children with ADHD often have other difficulties too

Children with ADHD are very likely to have other learning difficulties too. Dyspraxia (DCD) is the most common of the co-occurring learning difficulties (see Chapter 2), and the term DAMP (Deficit of Attention and Motor Perception) is used to describe children who have both ADHD and dyspraxia (see also page 40). More than 30 per cent of children with ADHD will have dyspraxia, while at least 35 per cent will have reading problems. (Since dyslexia and dyspraxia co-occur, some children will have all three problems.) That is why it is really important to make sure that your child is checked and receives help for *all* his or her difficulties.

The majority of children with ADHD (but not ADD) will have not only learning but also behavioural problems severe enough to attract a psychiatric diagnosis. The most common, affecting 60 per cent of youngsters diagnosed with ADHD, is what psychiatrists call Oppositional Defiant Disorder (ODD) – which basically means children do not do what they are told (most of the time, so the flavour is very different from normal 'stroppiness' and disobedience). Unfortunately, it is this behaviour that, *if not dealt with effectively*, can in the long run lead to more serious problems described by the umbrella term 'conduct disorder'. Conduct disorder means that the child behaves in antisocial ways – stealing, being physically violent with family members, getting into street fights, taking illegal drugs and being in trouble with the police are typical of the most troubled youngsters.

ADHD affects classroom learning

It is not the case that all children with ADHD have marked problems with their classroom achievements. However, learning *is* going to be much harder for children with ADHD – even for those who are bright. This is because they have a short concentration span; they don't listen to the teachers and so miss out on what is being said; they don't complete work in the time given; and they may well do their work in a slapdash and impulsive way. Of course, when children also have dyspraxia and dyslexia, learning will be even harder. So, *many* children with ADHD are likely to fall behind educationally.

Having said all this, there are some youngsters with ADHD who manage amazingly well. These are likely to be children with good language skills who have problems mainly with attention rather than long-standing hyperactivity, and who do not have co-occurring learning or behaviour difficulties. However, even those children who seem to manage and compensate reasonably well will still need teachers and parents to be aware of their attention problems, act positively and give structured support so they can fulfil their potential and be happy at school.

To find out whether your child has a significant problem with attention, fill in the questionnaire below and then do an observation, as described opposite.

GENERAL QUESTIONNAIRE:
COULD YOUR CHILD HAVE ADHD?

Does your child:

1. Have a very short concentration span?
Yes, definitely ❏   Yes, somewhat ❏   No ❏

2. Fidget and find it hard to sit still?
Yes, definitely ❏   Yes, somewhat ❏   No ❏

3. Act without thinking?
Yes, definitely ❏   Yes, somewhat ❏   No ❏

4. Fail to finish tasks once started (like homework, puzzles or household chores)?
Yes, definitely ❏   Yes, somewhat ❏   No ❏

5. Do dangerous things like run out into the road/lean out of windows/climb ladders or walls?
Yes, definitely ❏   Yes, somewhat ❏   No ❏

6. Blurt out things inappropriately?
Yes, definitely ❏   Yes, somewhat ❏   No ❏

7. Get easily distracted?
Yes, definitely ❏   Yes, somewhat ❏   No ❏

8. Spend a lot of time daydreaming when meant to be working?
Yes, definitely ❏   Yes, somewhat ❏   No ❏

9. Chatter and distract others at school?
Yes, definitely ❏   Yes, somewhat ❏   No ❏

10. Not listen to and/or take in instructions?
Yes, definitely ❑   Yes, somewhat ❑   No ❑

11. Regularly disrupt activities at home or school?
Yes, definitely ❑   Yes, somewhat ❑   No ❑

12. Have difficulty with timekeeping and meeting deadlines?
Yes, definitely ❑   Yes, somewhat ❑   No ❑

13. Need you to stand over him/her to get work done rather than getting on independently?
Yes, definitely ❑   Yes, somewhat ❑   No ❑

Results: General Questionnaire

If you answered 'Yes, definitely' to many items (and these behaviours have been evident for at least six months), then your child has significant problems with attention, impulsivity or level of activity. If you ticked mostly 'Yes, somewhat', there still might be some concerns. But bear in mind that many youngsters do have blips from time to time in their attention (especially as it is related to motivation). Also, they may behave differently at home and at school.

ATTENTION OBSERVATION (ALL AGES)

Now try a short *observation* of your child while doing homework. Watch from a little distance, so it is not obvious what you are doing. Observe 7–11 year olds for at least 15–20 minutes – and 12–14 year olds for 30 minutes (if you can!) Make some notes about what you see, then answer the following:

1. Did he/she take a very long time to settle down and start working?
Yes, definitely ❑   Yes, somewhat ❑   No ❑

2. Was he/she fidgety and restless – dropping things, doodling, wriggling in the chair, not able to sit still?
Yes, definitely ❑   Yes, somewhat ❑   No ❑

3. Did he/she frequently interrupt the work session – for instance, to go to the toilet, sharpen pencils or get a snack?
Yes, definitely ❑   Yes, somewhat ❑   No ❑

4. Did he/she give up on any task before finishing it?
Yes, definitely ❑   Yes, somewhat ❑   No ❑

5. Did he/she spend quite a bit of time not really doing anything, except staring into space (not apparently thinking about the homework)?
Yes, definitely ❑   Yes, somewhat ❑   No ❑

Results: Attention Observation (all ages)

Check out with your child's teacher whether what you have observed is happening at school. If you and the teacher agree that the answer in general is 'Yes, definitely' or even 'Yes, somewhat', then there are attention problems that need to be addressed.

THE WAY FORWARD

Knowing if a child has ADHD

Your answers to the questionnaires and your attention observation can be a guide, but deciding if a child has ADHD is complex and normally involves a professional consultation with a paediatrician, a child psychiatrist or a clinical psychologist. The professional will make a wide-ranging assessment before giving a formal diagnosis of ADHD. The assessment is likely to include:

■ A 'history' of past behaviour (what the child was like in the early years) as well as what is happening currently by getting information from both parents and teachers.

(Since children can behave very differently in different places – say home and school – it is vital to look at the child's behaviour 'across the board'. True ADHD will show itself across a wide range of situations and is not 'situation specific', seen in only one setting. Having said that, it is well known that most children with ADHD can contain themselves in novel situations, such as when taken along to see the GP or psychologist, or when doing self-chosen and usually undemanding activities like watching television.)

■ Direct observation of the child's behaviour. This is most often done by a clinical or educational psychologist in the classroom at school, and occasionally at home too.

■ Questionnaires and rating scales completed by parents and teachers. These can add extra information about how problematic the behaviours are in different situations.

■ Specific tests to assess different aspects of attention. These include the child's ability to *focus* regardless of outside distractions, the ability to *sustain attention* or 'keep going' over reasonably long periods of time, and the ability to *switch the focus of attention* from one activity to another swiftly when needed. Tests assist diagnosis by providing an objective measure of the child's behaviour and allowing a comparison of the child with others of the same age. They also allow the child's progress to be monitored by measuring changes in behaviour over time. Several measurements over a period of time can show whether treatments are effective or not. Many psychologists feel that tests of this sort are underused both for diagnosis and monitoring progress.

Coping with ADHD
To medicate or not to medicate?
This issue has attracted a lot of attention, particularly in the press, because not everyone agrees that drugs are a good solution for children. Some parents fear the use of medication because they don't like the idea of filling their children with 'chemicals'.

There has been a huge rise in the prescribing of medication for ADHD over the last few years. In 2006, 55,000 children in the UK were prescribed medication for attention difficulties, at a cost to the NHS of £28 million. The most usual medications are Ritalin and Concerta. Both of these are stimulants, creating 'highs' in adults. It may, therefore, seem surprising that in children these medications damp down impulsive and overactive behaviour while helping the child to focus. Ritalin, the most commonly prescribed of the drugs, is generally short acting and needs to be taken twice a day. Concerta, by contrast, is released more slowly into the bloodstream so its effects last all day without the need for a lunchtime top-up.

A recent study revealed that taking Ritalin over a number of years showed no long-term benefit on children's behaviour. This means that Ritalin may improve behaviour in the short term but these effects do not seem to last. Worryingly, many children showed a physical side-effect of slower growth rate. The National Institute for Health and Clinical Excellence (NICE) in the UK has now advised that drug therapy 'should only be part of a comprehensive treatment programme that includes a range of social, psychological and behavioural interventions'.

It is clear that children with ADHD require more than just medication to help them. If medication is to be used at all, it should be seen as a short-term strategy, opening up a window of opportunity for a child to develop new behaviour patterns, and for teachers and parents to get out of their cycle of criticism and (perfectly reasonable) feelings of despair.

Strategies for improving learning and behaviour
So, if not medication (or medication alone), then what? There are a number of strategies that teachers and other professionals can offer, such as:

■ Providing learning support within the classroom to help the child stay on task, complete work and stay out of trouble – for instance, by setting small, easily achievable targets and giving the child praise for each successful step along the way; having an agreed 'code' for reminding the child to get back on task, such as a tap on the desk; avoiding discussion of failures and faults.

■ Providing non-academic-related support in the form of 'social skills' training groups to help the child with ADHD relate better to others – by practising listening to others, taking turns, and learning to hold back and control anger and frustration better.

■ Helping parents *understand* their child's behaviour (and so not get caught up in a cycle of criticism).

■ Teaching parents to set up structured reward schemes for improving motivation to learn (see Chapter 11 for more ideas).

■ Recognising that the child with ADHD is very likely to have other specific learning difficulties (such as dyslexia and dyspraxia) that require specialist learning support in their own right; children will need formal psychological and educational assessments to make sure that none of their difficulties goes unrecognised and untreated.

■ Providing therapy and counselling for children with ADHD who have emotional problems.

Omega 3 supplements

Another treatment that is an appealing option to many parents is to give fish oils/omega 3 supplements. Studies by psychologist Dr Alex Richardson showed that (relatively) large doses did indeed lead to some improvements in concentration and motivation among children with mild to moderate attention problems. While there is some value in giving supplements, it is *not* a complete solution for most children with ADHD. (There have been claims for the effectiveness of fish oils in the treatment of dyslexia and dyspraxia also, but the evidence for this is far less convincing than for attention problems.) It is always unwise for children to be given supplements without consulting your doctor first, as you do not want your child to take too large a dose.

Food additives and colourings

The link between food additives (and colourings) and ADHD has attracted a lot of attention from both the media and from parents who are convinced that their child's hyperactive behaviour is due to the additives contained in many sweets and fizzy drinks. The research evidence for food additives causing overactivity has largely been unconvincing, with some studies showing some links and others showing none at all. In a recent study by Professor Jim Stevenson from Southampton University, groups of three year olds and eight year olds were given a special 'treatment drink'; half the children had an additive-free fruit juice while the other half had a drink containing a mixture of food colourings and preservatives. Professor Stevenson found that some children's behaviour was made worse by certain food colours and preservatives. He concluded: 'The finding lends strong support for the case that food additives exacerbate hyperactive behaviours (inattention, impulsivity and overactivity) at least into middle childhood.' He added: 'Parents should not think that simply taking these additives out of food will prevent all hyperactive disorders. We know that many other influences are at work but this at least is one a child can avoid.'

What happens later to children with ADHD?

In reality, most children with full-blown ADHD do not outgrow their problems by early to middle childhood. Many will have difficulties that persist throughout their childhood and even their adult lives. Of course, what happens in the future for any individual depends on the number and degree of severity of problems the child has to cope with. It also depends on how early these have been recognised and understood, and how effectively they have been dealt with. Fortunately, ADHD is now recognised as a common specific learning difficulty with much less stigma attached to it than in previous years. More is known about ADHD and its impact, and also about the other learning, behaviour, social and emotional problems that can go alongside it. Parents and teachers working together throughout the school years will go a long way to ensure that children's problems are recognised and helped at every stage.

■　■　■

ADHD is a severe specific learning difficulty affecting many aspects of behaviour: attention, impulsivity and hyperactivity. ADD is a less severe problem but it can also affect children's progress in learning, as well as their friendships and self-esteem. ADD is probably under-recognised as a problem, with many such children being told only that they 'must learn to concentrate'. ADHD is more easily spotted, but mostly in boys – so care needs to be taken not to overlook the problem in girls. Drug treatments, once seen as the wonder solution, may offer only temporary benefits and may have worrying side-effects. Effective management strategies for ADHD need to deal with all aspects of a child's life – behavioural, social, emotional as well as learning.

If the results of the questionnaire and your own observations point to your child having an attention difficulty, you will need to talk this through with the teacher. Also look at the strategies outlined in Chapters 10 and 11 for practical suggestions on what you can do to improve your child's concentration.

5

Could Your Child Have Dyscalculia?

'Specific maths difficulty' and 'dyscalculia' can be considered to be one and the same thing. So little is known about maths difficulties that it makes sense to use the terms interchangeably. The word 'dyscalculia' simply means 'disorder of an ability to calculate'. Some children will do poorly at maths however, not because they have a specific difficulty, but because of problems with behaviour, bad teaching, missing lessons and anxiety about maths.

Dyscalculia is usually defined as a level of mathematical ability well below that expected for the child's age and intelligence. Children with dyscalculia, but also children with maths problems due to other causes, are likely to show the following:

- Difficulty in doing mental arithmetic.
- Making errors in simple written sums.
- Finding it hard to understand and to remember number concepts and procedures.
- Difficulty in coping with maths problem solving.
- Inability to remember number bonds and reliance on finger counting (or even guessing!)
- Slowness to learn times tables (and speed in forgetting them).

Children with dyscalculia have been shown to be different from children with generally poor maths in that they have fundamental problems in the understanding of simple number concepts. The underlying causes of dyscalculia are far less well understood than those of dyslexia, but Professor Brian Butterworth, a psychologist who is an authority on maths, has recently shown that children with dyscalculia:

- have great difficulty learning to count
- find it hard to select which is the larger of two numbers
- cannot easily 'subitise' (that is, they are unable to look at a small number of objects on a page and say how many there are without actually counting them)

DYSCALCULIA QUIZ

Find out how much you already know about dyscalculia. Read each statement and circle TRUE or FALSE, then look at the following pages for the answers and more information.

1. Dyscalculia is as common as dyslexia.   TRUE or FALSE

2. Many more boys than girls have dyscalculia.

TRUE or FALSE

3. Maths problems are much less likely to be inherited than reading problems.   TRUE or FALSE

4. Reading involves more complicated skills than maths.

TRUE or FALSE

5. Children with maths problems have difficulty storing number facts in their long-term memory.   TRUE or FALSE

6. Visual-spatial problems underlie maths difficulties in many children.   TRUE or FALSE

7. Maths problems can't be prevented.   TRUE or FALSE

Now how did you do?

1. *Dyscalculia is as common as dyslexia.* **TRUE**
2. *Many more boys than girls have dyscalculia.* **FALSE**
3. *Maths problems are much less likely to be inherited than reading problems.* **FALSE**
4. *Reading involves more complicated skills than maths.* **FALSE**
5. *Children with maths problems have difficulty storing number facts in their long-term memory.* **TRUE**
6. *Visual-spatial problems underlie maths difficulties in many children.* **TRUE**
7. *Maths problems can't be prevented.* **TRUE and FALSE**

FACTS ABOUT DYSCALCULIA

Dyscalculia – a common but little-understood problem

If you were 'bad at maths' at school, you probably would have accepted that and got on with the rest of the subjects – and the rest of your life. Reading, on the other hand, has long been seen as central to all aspects of education – if you can't read, you can't do any subject at school and are regarded as 'illiterate and uneducated'. Perhaps it is for this reason that less research has been directed at maths, with the result that dyscalculia is far less well understood than dyslexia. It is harder, therefore, to get the true figures on just how common maths difficulties are – and what types of problems these children have.

Overall, studies have shown that difficulties in maths are nearly as common as those of reading. The figure seems to be around 6 per cent of children, with roughly equal numbers of boys and girls having maths difficulties. This makes dyscalculia the one learning difficulty that affects boys and girls equally.

Dyscalculia is inherited

Dyscalculia – just as much as dyslexia (and dyspraxia) – runs in families. It therefore has a strong genetic basis. There is some evidence that dyscalculia can be associated with a defect on the X (female) chromosome, which explains why girls with Turner's syndrome who have three, as opposed to the usual two, X chromosomes have considerable difficulties in maths.

Professor Brian Butterworth is convinced that there is a specialised numerical facility in the brain. Evidence for this comes from research that looks at the link between maths ability and the results of brain scans. The part of the brain known as the parietal lobes (on each side of the brain just above the ears) seems to be where maths skills are positioned. A study by psychologist Dr Elizabeth Isaacs of University College London has shown that children who are born prematurely have difficulty with doing basic sums. The scans on these children showed that they had fewer cells in the parietal lobe on the left side of the brain, in a very precise spot called the intra-parietal sulcus.

Maths is a complex skill

Maths involves more – and more complex – skills than reading. People may find that rather surprising. The skills needed for reading accurately are primarily phonological (speech sound) abilities and learning to decode. Maths is dependent on a wider range of skills: **short-term working memory**, storage of number facts in **long-term memory**, **counting** and **understanding number size**, **visual-spatial skills** and **planning and organisation**.

■ *Short-term (or working) memory* is important for mental arithmetic because children have to be able to 'hold' numbers in their head and carry out the calculation at the same time. Mental calculations are also needed for written maths. Studies have shown that many children with dyscalculia have trouble with this kind of memory.

■ *An ability to store number facts* is needed for retaining and recalling number concepts and the operational procedures that have already been taught for doing sums. Number bonds and multiplication tables have to be remembered over the long term and recalled easily (without having to resort to finger counting). Number facts have to be permanently represented in the long-term memory. This is rather like a large storage box – very different to the on-line system of short-term memory where the information stays only if it is constantly repeated and so 'refreshed'. There is some evidence that children with dyscalculia have difficulties storing number facts and procedures in their long-term memory – it's not clear yet whether the main problem is of getting the information into the store in the first place, keeping it there or getting it out (recalling it).

■ *Counting* skills are important because they underpin addition and subtraction. For very young children, adding means 'counting up from' and subtracting means 'counting down from'. Children with dyscalculia find it very hard to learn to count accurately, and even when they are much older they are still very slow at counting. Many experts in the maths field agree that an underlying difficulty resulting in counting problems is the inability to *represent number magnitudes* – which means that children with dyscalculia find it hard to connect a number such as '5' to 'fiveness'. This may well be the reason why they have trouble with number comparisons – they can't easily and quickly say that 32 is bigger than 23.

■ *Visual-spatial skills* are important for learning about the many visual concepts in maths. Geometry is obviously visual, but there are other aspects of maths that depend on visual skills – keeping numbers in their columns while doing written sums, understanding fractions and decimals as being 'parts of a whole', 'reading' and interpreting figures on graphs and grid tables, and so on. Studies have shown that many children with dyscalculia find it hard to do puzzles, which suggests that they have visual-spatial problems.

■ *Planning and organisation* are needed because, for many maths questions, the child has to carry out a series of ordered steps to arrive at the answer. This is particularly true for problem solving maths – something that many children with dyscalculia find difficult. Maths problem- solving is very complicated because, first of all, children have to understand what the question is asking them to do overall. Second, they have to be able to decide what steps need to be taken and in what order. Finally, the steps have each to be 'translated' into a sum (or numerical operation). Keeping track of all these steps involves what we have described for ADHD as an 'executive function' (see page 83). This is one reason why maths is more complex than reading, which does not have such a clear-cut executive component.

Some children with dyscalculia might have problems with all the above, while others might have difficulties with some but not others. Does this mean there are different *types* of dyscalculia, or do children with all the above problems just have a more severe version of dyscalculia than those with some problems? There is no clear answer to this at the moment.

Could your child have dyscalculia? Complete the General Questionnaire to look at how things are now. Next, complete the Early Signs Questionnaire to remind yourself of your child's early progress in number work.

GENERAL QUESTIONNAIRE: COULD YOUR CHILD HAVE DYSCALCULIA?

How is your child doing *now*? Does he/she:

1. Have trouble learning new concepts in maths?
Yes, definitely ❏   Yes, somewhat ❏   No ❏

2. Still find it hard to remember the basic number bonds to 10 (e.g. 1+9=10, 7+3=10, 5+5=10) without having to think about it or count on fingers?
Yes, definitely ❏   Yes, somewhat ❏   No ❏

3. Make lots of errors when carrying out calculations?
Yes, definitely ❏   Yes, somewhat ❏   No ❏

4. Get confused while working with 10s and units?

Yes, definitely ❑   Yes, somewhat ❑   No ❑

5. Forget what type of sum is being done while in the middle of doing it (e.g. switches from takeaway to addition halfway through the sum)?

Yes, definitely ❑   Yes, somewhat ❑   No ❑

6. Work very slowly when doing calculations?

Yes, definitely ❑   Yes, somewhat ❑   No ❑

7. Have a lot of difficulty remembering how to do the basic number operations, particularly subtraction with 'borrowing' and 'payback', long division and long multiplication?

Yes, definitely ❑   Yes, somewhat ❑   No ❑

8. Get anxious about maths, dislike it, and feel 'rubbish' at it?

Yes, definitely ❑   Yes, somewhat ❑   No ❑

EARLY SIGNS QUESTIONNAIRE

As a pre-schooler, did your child:

1. Have difficulty learning to count?

Yes, definitely ❑   Yes, somewhat ❑   No ❑

2. Take a long time to learn how to compare numbers, that is to say which is the *bigger* or *smaller* of two numbers – for instance 4 is bigger than 2, 3 is smaller than 5?

Yes, definitely ❑   Yes, somewhat ❑   No ❑

3. Have difficulty learning to continue a pattern – like red, yellow, blue; red, yellow ____ (answer: blue)?

Yes, definitely ❑   Yes, somewhat ❑   No ❑

4. Have trouble learning to write the numbers 1 to 9?
Yes, definitely ❑   Yes, somewhat ❑   No ❑

5. Find it hard to learn the language of measurement, such as longer-shorter, heavier-lighter, bigger-smaller, full-empty, thick-thin, more-less …?
Yes, definitely ❑   Yes, somewhat ❑   No ❑

Results: General and Early Signs Questionnaires

If you answered 'Yes, definitely' to most of the questions in the General Questionnaire, and 'Yes, definitely' (or even 'Yes, somewhat') to most of the questions in the Early Signs Questionnaire, your child's difficulties and worries are worth following up. Try also the checks below.

The first two items in the Early Signs Questionnaire are known to be *markers* (or key signs) of a specific maths difficulty or dyscalculia. The first marker is oral and written counting skill. The second marker is the ability to make fast judgements between pairs of numbers (saying which of the two is the bigger number).

YOUR OWN CHECKS

Maths markers (for all ages)

Counting
Ask your child to count out loud (forwards) from 1 to 30.
Then ask him/her to count backwards from 30 down to 1.
Finally, ask your child to write down the numbers 1 to 50 (for 7–11 year olds) or 1 to 100 (for ages 12–14).

Comparing number size
Show your child these pairs of numbers one at a time (a ruler or plain sheet of paper would do the job of hiding the next pair of numbers). Ask him/her to tell you or point to the *bigger* of the two numbers.

68	51
34	49
72	58
16	61
73	37

Results: Maths markers

If your child makes errors and/or is very slow on either or both of these maths markers, then he or she is showing the signs typical of an underlying maths difficulty.

Sums: The different operations

Now check how well your child can manage some basic sums. Before you start, remind your child to check the (operation) signs carefully and keep the answers out of your child's sight.

For ages 7–8

$$26 \qquad 37$$
$$+13 \qquad -24$$

$$3 \times 7 =$$

$$6 \times 5 =$$

$$2\,\sqrt{8}$$

$$3\,\sqrt{18}$$

For ages 9–11

$$58 \atop +25$$

$$90 \atop -47$$

$$26 \atop \times\ 3$$

$$37 \atop \times\ 6$$

$$4\sqrt{48}$$

$$5\sqrt{530}$$

For ages 12–14

$$372 \atop 816 \atop +245$$

$$617 \atop -359$$

$$35 \atop \times\ 24$$

$$23.0 \atop \times\ 0.6$$

$$7\sqrt{931}$$

$$12\sqrt{1425}$$

For each age group do make up some more similar sums of your own if you are not sure whether these are enough to give a clear picture of your child's level.

Results: Sums

Here are the answers for you to check against.

For ages 7–8

$$26 \atop +13 \atop \overline{39}$$

$$37 \atop -24 \atop \overline{13}$$

3 x 7 = **21**

6 x 5 = **30**

$$2\sqrt{8}^{\,4} \qquad 3\sqrt{18}^{\,6}$$

For ages 9–11

58	90	26	37
+25	−47	x 3	x 6
83	**43**	**78**	**222**

$$4\overline{)48} = 12 \qquad 5\overline{)530} = 106$$

For ages 12–14

372			
816	617	35	23.0
+245	−359	x 24	x 0.6
1433	**258**	**840**	**13.8**

$$7\overline{)931} = 133 \qquad 12\overline{)1425} = 118\ r9 \quad \text{or} \quad 12\overline{)1425} = 118.75$$

Your child should be able to do the sums in this section without error. If your child was fine on the marker tests but made some errors on the sums, then perhaps a little extra help with calculation methods and practice with work sheets will be enough to help gain skills and confidence.

If your child made errors on the sums *and also* had problems with the two marker items, then he or she is having significant maths difficulties that need following up.

THE WAY FORWARD

Assessing number problems

Screening and assessment for dyscalculia are not currently done at school routinely. However, children's level of number skill is assessed by the national tests at Key Stages 1–3, which may help to flag up whether a child is having a problem with maths. The test results will only show whether a child is up to class standard in maths, not whether they have a selective or specific difficulty that might be called dyscalculia.

There has been some interest of late in the development of

dyscalculia screening tests. Although these are not yet routinely used, there are several simple checks that look to be very promising screening tools:

- Counting accurately and quickly, especially for the higher numbers (and in particular counting in twos).
- Comparing number magnitudes – being able to say accurately and quickly which of two (either spoken or written) numbers is the bigger.
- Saying both accurately and quickly how many dots (between four and six) there are on a sheet of paper or a computer screen.

Children referred to specialist teachers or psychologists are usually given standardised tests that assess their maths knowledge in relation to children of the same age. This would involve doing pencil and paper sums of increasing difficulty, covering the basic number operations of addition, subtraction, multiplication and division – including whole numbers, fractions and decimals. Children should also be assessed on a test of mathematical reasoning and understanding of number concepts.

Further testing could also involve specific assessments for dyscalculia. Commercially available measures to assess whether a child's maths difficulties are indeed due to dyscalculia have now been developed. Professor Butterworth's 'Dyslexia Screener' is designed to separate true dyscalculia from low attainment in arithmetic. This contains tasks such as dot counting and number comparisons. These measures are the equivalent of using phonological processing and non-word (nonsense) reading tests to identify dyslexia.

A comprehensive assessment of dyscalculia should include tests of verbal and nonverbal skills, standardised maths tests, some diagnostic tests, background history and behavioural measures of attention. This information can be put together to decide whether the child's maths problems are caused by dyscalculia or by other factors like poor teaching, lack of attention or low motivation. The tests should also show what sorts of maths difficulties the child is having – for instance, geometry and symmetry or basic calculations or problem solving … or everything.

Maths difficulties can sometimes be prevented

A child born with a brain that is not well geared up for maths is going to find this subject very difficult. Obviously, you can't help what you are born with. However, if children likely to have maths problems are identified at the very beginning, then much can be done to teach them skills that will help stop them falling behind. Early recognition, together with assessment in the primary years, will help to identify what specific underlying difficulties an individual child has (whether, for example, these are memory or visual-spatial problems). Armed with this information, teachers can set up a learning plan tailored to the child's particular difficulties and needs. It is important that children do not miss out on the early foundation concepts in maths, as each stage in maths learning depends on the earlier stage being understood and 'fixed' permanently. Learning maths is a bit like building a brick wall; the foundations and bottom rows hold the whole structure in place.

Early intervention is also important to reduce worry and anxiety in children about their maths performance. Anxiety about maths is very common and can all too readily make children panic as they wrestle with their sums. Children with dyscalculia have been shown to have particular worries about doing maths tests and exams, and also about doing specific computations like long division. They may stop trying altogether or just write down 'any old thing' in a desperate hope to show their teachers that they are at least making an effort. But such strategies inevitably lead to failure as their work becomes full of even more errors – and motivation and self-confidence in their abilities plummet.

With the study of dyscalculia still in its early days, it is not surprising to learn that there are virtually no research studies that have systematically looked at whether some maths teaching programmes are more effective than others. In the UK, special maths programmes for children with dyscalculia are at last being developed for use in schools (see also Resources). Parents can additionally do much at home to pick up difficulties as well as practise and reinforce maths concepts and skills (see Chapter 10).

■ ■ ■

Dyscalculia is a specific learning disability that is largely inherited, due to the way a certain part of the brain – the parietal lobes – has developed. It is an even more complex learning difficulty than dyslexia because so many skills are involved: short- and long-term memory, visual-spatial skills, counting skills, and planning and organisation abilities. Dyscalculia has also, until recently, been largely overlooked. Early intervention is essential to prevent maths difficulties as well as the anxieties that go with this for many children and their parents.

Now you have completed all the questionnaires and checks, you should have a good idea whether or not there are concerns about your child's learning or educational progress that are worth following up. The next step is to go to your child's school to talk to the teachers.

6

Overlapping Learning Difficulties

Dyslexia, dyspraxia, and problems with language, maths and attention can exist on their own – that is, separately and in 'pure' form. But they can, and very often do, occur side by side in various combinations. This is what is known as **co-morbidity** or **co-occurrence**.

When parents think about why their children are struggling with learning at school, it is tempting to look for a single answer. This could be a mistake. There is an increasing awareness amongst professionals and academics that if a child has a particular learning difficulty, there is a strong likelihood that there will be other learning difficulties occurring alongside it. In the 'at risk' study described in Chapter 1, 70 per cent of the children with dyslexia had at least one other type of learning difficulty too – frequently maths, but sometimes also nonverbal difficulties, attention or language problems. It is increasingly recognised that a pure or single learning difficulty is the exception rather than the rule. That is why it is very important to make sure children with a suspected learning difficulty are given a very thorough assessment covering a wide range of learning and educational skills. Failure to spot other learning difficulties may result in the child not receiving the best possible understanding and help.

CO-OCCURRENCE – JUST AN UNLUCKY ACCIDENT?

Having one specific learning difficulty is tough enough, but having two or more seems most unfair and is doubly frustrating. Two learning difficulties mean that two sets of teaching strategies have to be set up. Sometimes more than double the effort is required from the child (and parents too!)

Is co-occurrence just an unlucky accident? The evidence suggests mostly not. Co-occurrence is so common that it could not happen by chance. So if it doesn't happen by chance then what is the reason for it?

From brain to classroom

To help understand co-occurrence, it is useful to look first at the different levels of explanation for any one type of learning difficulty. There are three levels:

1. The **biological** level. Learning difficulties are likely to be associated with several different genes. Genes are best not seen as 'causes' of learning problems; rather they create risks for the child of developing them. The more risks, the more likely it is that there will be learning problems. And the more types of risks, the more severe the overall problems are likely to be – so it will be harder to overcome them. In the case of dyslexia, a child with both language and phonological difficulties (two risks) will have more problems than a child with poor phonology but good language. The biological level of explanation also refers to those parts of the brain that are relevant for a particular learning difficulty – for instance, parts of the left side of the brain are affected in children with language impairment.

2. The **cognitive** level. This refers to the underlying skills that are important for learning – such as memory, phonological processing, spatial ability and so on.

3. The **behavioural** level. This refers to the educational effects of the underlying cognitive difficulty, such as problems with reading, writing or the ability to stay on task in the classroom (attention).

There is one further level that makes a big difference to how the other three levels can affect any one child – and that is the **environment**. Examples of how each level can interact with the environment to cause learning difficulties are:

- At the **biological** level a mother drinking alcohol during pregnancy can result in damage to her child's brain – and a condition known as foetal alcohol syndrome.
- At the **cognitive** level, if children at risk for dyslexia have lots of good language stimulation – especially work on phonological games – in the pre-school years, it may reduce the severity of the reading difficulties they are likely to have.
- At the **behavioural** or educational level, again for children at risk of dyslexia, spotting the problems in the early school years and giving appropriate literacy teaching and support at school (and at home too) will do much to help them compensate for their difficulties.

The picture is slightly more complicated because not only does the environment shape biology, cognition and behaviour, but these in turn affect the environment. For instance, pre-schoolers with a language difficulty could have problems forming friendships in the nursery school environment because communication is very hard for them. School-age children with a learning difficulty may end up with teachers being cross because they seem 'lazy' or 'careless' and hide their work or don't do it. Many children feel badly about their difficulties, and their emotional state affects their ability to learn.

Don't miss overlapping learning difficulties
Two learning difficulties may co-occur because they share the *same underlying cause* or causes. For instance, SLI and dyslexia share some of the same underlying cognitive difficulties. At the biology level, some of the same genes and nearby parts of the left side of the brain will be involved in these two difficulties. At the cognitive level, there will be shared problems of phonological processing and maybe also short-term verbal memory.

SLI and dyslexia might look like this in a given child:

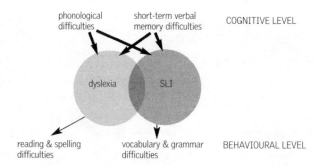

The *shared* learning difficulties are shown by the shaded part where the circles overlap. The thick arrows at the cognitive level show shared causes.. At the behavioural level, the thin arrows show what language and educational difficulties result.

Dyscalculia and dyslexia are two learning difficulties that may also co-occur due to shared genes and, therefore, shared causes. Children who have both these learning difficulties very often have short-term verbal memory problems. An efficient short-term or immediate verbal working memory is important for making arithmetic calculations and for remembering sequences of sounds in words. The thick arrows show the shared causes. There are also some non-shared causes: phonological difficulties cause dyslexia, and spatial problems cause dyscalculia (these are shown by the thin arrows at the cognitive level).

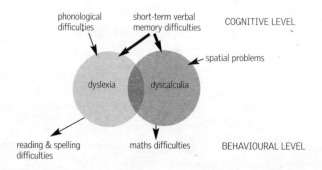

Some learning difficulties seem to *cluster* together on a regular basis, but with no clear joint underlying cause or reason. Dyslexia and dyspraxia are two learning difficulties that very often go together. These children have reading and spelling difficulties and also problems with handwriting, organisation, presentation and maybe even sports. They are likely to be slow to complete work, so timed examinations can be a nightmare.

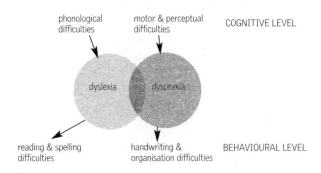

Another common cluster is DAMP (Deficit of Attention and Motor Perception, see page 40). Children with DAMP have an attention deficit together with visual perception difficulties and problems of fine, and sometimes gross, motor control. They not only have trouble concentrating on their school work, but also have difficulty with handwriting, may be poorly co-ordinated in sport and typically have great problems of organisation and presentation of work. Some children with a severe version of DAMP have speech difficulties, as they find it hard to control and co-ordinate the muscles and organs of speech.

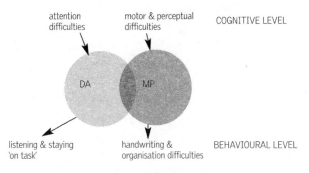

A very small number of children have three, and sometimes four, co-occurring learning difficulties. These are the children whose difficulties are so complex and severe that they may need to attend a special school.

To make it easier to understand what happens to children when learning difficulties co-occur, read about one child from our casebook.

Kelly

Kelly was 10 and a half when she was brought for assessment by her parents. They had long-standing concerns about her difficulty with maths. More recently, her teachers had said that her reading and spelling were behind that of other children in her class. Kelly's teachers filled in a questionnaire showing that she had no concentration or behaviour problems but was beginning to show signs of frustration and of feeling demoralised about her lack of progress.

Since she was six years old, Kelly had been receiving additional learning support at school. The school's special needs teacher worked with her on a catch-up numeracy programme, and a teaching assistant heard her read two or three times a week. Her parents also arranged for her to have one-to-one teaching outside school every fortnight. Kelly's early developmental history was normal. Her father recalled that he had a lot of difficulty with maths when younger.

During the test, Kelly concentrated hard, was positive and eager to please and engaged well. In an ability (IQ) test she achieved an above-average verbal IQ of 119, in the top 10 per cent for her age group. She had a lot more difficulty with the test of nonverbal IQ, obtaining a score of only 79, placing her visual learning skills in the bottom 10 per cent for her age group. The discrepancy between the verbal and nonverbal IQs was a huge 40 points. This indicated that, although Kelly was clearly very bright verbally, she had difficulties with nonverbal or visual learning. (This is the sort of discrepancy expected in children who have nonverbal learning difficulties or dyspraxia.) Interestingly, although Kelly had perceptual and spatial problems, she did not have any obvious fine motor difficulties. She was able to draw well (art was her favourite subject at school), she scored slightly above age level on a pencil-and-paper copying test, and her handwriting was nicely formed and clearly legible.

Kelly's maths was very poor. She was given two maths tests; one was a pencil-and-paper test that looked at her understanding of the four basic arithmetic operations, while the other was geared towards maths reasoning, understanding of number concepts and problem solving. Kelly's maths skills were at the level of an average seven to eight year old and in the bottom 5 per cent for her age group. Kelly could manage addition with carrying over but only basic subtraction, multiplication and division. She could not tell the time or read a simple graph. She could not say which number in a sequence was the biggest, and the fractions and geometry sums were beyond her.

Not only was Kelly struggling in maths, but she was also having difficulty with reading and spelling. In both a single word reading test and one in which she had to read stories, her reading accuracy was found to be at around the nine to nine and a half year level – about 12 to 18 months below her chronological age and in the bottom 25 per cent for her age group. Her reading comprehension matched her reading accuracy. But Kelly had particular difficulty with decoding; she struggled with a nonsense word reading test, scoring at the level of an average six year old and in the bottom 5 per cent for her age group. She was showing the real word/nonsense word discrepancy typical of children with dyslexia – that is, her real word reading was well ahead of her nonsense word reading. Not surprisingly, Kelly was a poor speller. On a spelling test, she scored at the level of an average eight year old. Her spelling errors showed that she 'simplified' words – so she wrote 'rough' as 'ruff' and 'whistle' as 'wisel'.

Further testing was done to see if Kelly had underlying phonological processing and short-term verbal memory difficulties that are usually seen in children with dyslexia. On a digit span test (a test of immediate memory for numbers), Kelly scored at about the six-year level, and on a test of phonological processing (deleting sounds from spoken words), she scored at around the eight-year level.

Kelly had both dyslexia and dyscalculia. Her dyslexia was caused by her poor phonological processing and her limited short-term verbal memory. These in turn affected her ability to learn to decode – and so she had fallen behind in reading and spelling. Kelly had co-occurring dyscalculia. This seemed to have two causes. First, her short-term verbal memory difficulties were affecting her mental maths (and resulting in the overlap of Kelly's dyslexia and dyscalculia because they cause problems in both literacy and maths). Second, she had perceptual and spatial weaknesses that were making it hard for her to understand visual concepts in maths like fractions, geometry and interpreting graphs. Kelly's dyscalculia seemed to be inherited from her father, who had always found maths difficult.

■ ■ ■

The main message here is you need to be prepared to spot more than just one problem. Understanding the different levels that affect a learning difficulty will help you to see where your child's problems are coming from. Assessments covering a wide range of skills (at the levels of cognition and behaviour) are needed to describe your child's difficulties fully. Knowing all this will make a difference to what action you take – and will make sure that none of your child's difficulties are missed.

How Professionals Can Help

7

Getting Help from School

Getting help from school is likely to be the first action to take once you are concerned that your child might have a specific learning difficulty. This is best done through the class teacher in the primary school and through the form tutor in the secondary school. There are some good ways to approach this – and others that may not be helpful. Here is our advice.

WORKING WITH TEACHERS

Listen carefully to the teacher's concerns, which may be different from yours. For example, you may be worried about your child's progress in maths while the teacher sees the problem as one of poor attention and general behaviour in maths lessons. Remember that any learning difficulty a child might have is likely to have an effect on other aspects of school life – including relationships with other children as well as teachers, and behaviour in general.

Aim towards a good *partnership* with your child's school so that you can work together. How the teachers see *you* could affect how they treat and respond to your child. If they think you're being critical of their teaching skills or personal qualities, they may become defensive and try to find excuses or even blame you and your child. This in turn could make it harder for them to take on board what you're trying to get across. An example of how *not* to approach school is to announce that you have 'diagnosed' your child as 'dyslexic' (and school has missed it).

Try not to bombard teachers when they are preoccupied and busy. Ask for a meeting time convenient for you both when there is time to talk. That way you will both be more relaxed, and it will be easier to share views and observations. Don't take babies or toddlers along with you to meetings as they will make it hard for you to get your points across. Bring a partner or friend if you want some moral support.

Before you meet up with a teacher, write down a list of the concerns you have about your child's learning. Use the information from the questionnaires you filled in and the checks you carried out yourself as the basis for your discussion. Best of all, bring in the results of these and show them to the teacher.

Know what school can do to help

You and the teachers can then work together on planning the next step. The school will be able to provide a lot of help – both from the class teacher and teaching assistants, and perhaps from the Special Educational Needs Co-ordinator (SENCO) (see opposite), or even visiting specialist teachers. Discuss with school whether further *assessment* could lead to a better understanding of your child's difficulties. This might take the form of an assessment by the SENCO or by other specialists (see Chapter 8). Neither a formal assessment nor help from school for your child is one-sided, that is, only the school's job. There is much you can do at home (see Chapters 10 and 11).

What can happen next?

There are various actions that can be taken following your first meeting at school.

Watch and talk

You and the teacher might want to find out more about your child's difficulties with learning.

In the primary school, this could largely take the form of the teachers *watching* your child in class, *looking at all his or her books* and *talking about his or her behaviour* with other staff. At this stage, children are already receiving **Quality First Teaching** (which is what **Wave 1**, the first step in Special Educational Needs, provides, see diagram overleaf). This means that the class teacher is aiming to meet the needs of children of all abilities through whole class teaching and through providing daily maths and literacy hour teaching.

In the secondary school, reports on your child's work and also his or her behaviour would need to be gathered from all the individual subject teachers.

Ask the teacher how much time is needed to gather this information before you take things further. Up to two weeks might be reasonable – try to be patient!

Watch and keep track

Maybe all that is needed for the time being is keeping a close eye on your child and recording progress. It is likely that your child's – and all children's – progress in school is already being tracked. In some schools, the Key Stage levels will be noted on a grid, and if your child is clearly failing to progress, there will be a recognised need to intervene anyway. This tracking may well be done by the assistant head. You as a parent could request to see how your child has progressed. Writing a special, more detailed record of learning and behaviour is another way for the teacher to monitor progress. Test or examination results, school reports or further comments from other teachers are additional ways. You will no doubt want to keep in close touch with the school to see how the special record monitoring is going.

There are two possible outcomes from the monitoring: the feedback you receive may reassure you that all is well. Alternatively, you and the teacher may decide that you need to take further action. This would normally start with involving the SENCO and/or other professionals.

Involve the SENCO

Calling on the SENCO is likely to be the first suggestion made by the teacher. Each school has an assigned teacher (the SENCO) who takes responsibility for special needs throughout the school. The SENCO's job is to consider, together with the class teacher, which children require extra support. These children are placed on the **Special Needs Register** (sometimes known as the **Inclusion Register***). The SENCO may want to carry out additional tests or checks to help decide whether the child should be put on the Register.

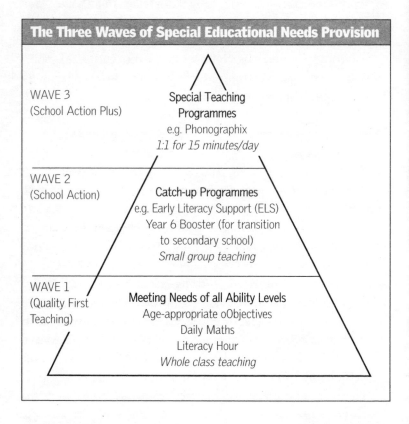

It is usual to put the child first on a needs level known as **School Action** (which is **Wave 2** of special needs provision, see diagram above). In the School Action/Wave 2 phase your child's progress

---

* Some schools also have an Inclusions Officer who, confusingly, can be either the SENCO or a different member of staff. The Inclusions Officer's job is to make sure that all children have equal access to the National Curriculum. This means that, however great a child's learning difficulties are, the *goal* is for the child to be able to learn the same subjects as the rest of the year group and participate fully in normal school life.

continues to be monitored, and additional learning support should be provided. School Action/Wave 2 **Catch-up Programmes** will be offered. These are designed to help with particular learning difficulties and are for pupils who can be expected to 'catch up' with their peers with a little extra help. They consist of short, scripted programmes (that is, programmes with a preset worded plan so they can be delivered by someone who is not a fully trained teacher). The features of Catch-up Programmes are:

- They are small-group based (around six to eight children).
- They are run by a learning support assistant (LSA), except for one lesson per week which is run by the class teacher, and they usually take place outside the classroom.
- They last for 20–30 minutes at a time and are delivered up to five times per week.
- They are aimed at children who are slightly underachieving (those with severe difficulties wouldn't be able to manage or 'access' them).
- The class teacher (not the LSA) remains in overall charge of the programme and of the progress of the children.
- If progress over a period of time on School Action/Wave 2 is slow (likely to be defined as inadequate response to two Catch-up Programmes over a year, though sometimes extending to two or even three years), the SENCO and teacher are likely to recommend moving your child on to the next level.

School Action Plus forms **Wave 3** and is the next level of Special Educational Needs. In this phase your child will receive a formal **Individual Education Plan (IEP)** (sometimes known as an Inclusion Provision Map) (see page 126 for an example). Sometimes IEPs are offered at School Action, but only at School Action Plus are specific targets set. These are set by the SENCO, who is not usually involved to the same degree at School Action. At School Action Plus, referrals may be made to outside school agencies such as psychologists and speech and language therapists. Additionally, at School Action Plus the child should receive a higher level of support than at School Action. In most Local (Education) Authorities this will typically involve special teaching programmes that are given one-to-one for 15 minutes per day.

An IEP is a very good way for teachers to plan and communicate to parents, other teachers and outside school professionals their ideas of action for a particular child. These IEPs are likely to be constructed slightly differently in individual schools but they should cover the same key elements. Nearly all have:

- **targets** that the child will need help to achieve (at School Action Plus only)
- **learning support strategies** that need to be put in place for the child to reach their targets
- **criteria** for successful achievement of the targets
- a section to **record** the date on which the criteria were met – or failed to be met

Some IEPs will contain additional information such as:

- test results (usually from formal assessments by specialist professionals or from teachers)
- profiles of the child's strengths and weaknesses gathered from various sources
- a needs section that defines in a more general way what the targets describe more specifically
- barriers to learning such as a hearing impairment or not having English as a first language

Many schools now hold an **Inclusion Surgery** to discuss all children who are on the Special Needs Register. This is a termly meeting of the SENCO together with the class teacher, LSA and sometimes others from outside agencies. At these meetings each child's individual needs are discussed and an IEP drawn up.

Involve other professionals

The involvement of other professionals such as **educational** (and sometimes **clinical**) **psychologists**, **speech and language thera-pists**, **occupational therapists**, **physiotherapists**, **paediatricians** and **psychiatrists** will largely depend on the kind of problem your child has and how much difficulty it is causing. This is only likely to be arranged by school if your child is on School Action Plus, but you can take independent action outside school if you wish.

If your child has mainly *literacy* or *maths* problems that are not improving as a result of the additional learning support (see above), then referral to a psychologist for a more detailed assess-ment could well be recommended.

If your child has difficulties with *speech and language*, then it would be a good idea to discuss whether a referral to a speech and language therapist would be helpful. This kind of referral may need to be made via your GP. You will have to be prepared, unfortunately, for the fact that speech and language resources are very limited. It may be hard to obtain an assessment – and even harder to get ongoing therapy – once a child is over five.

Occupational therapists, and sometimes physiotherapists, will be called upon to do detailed assessments for children with *nonverbal* and/or *fine motor problems*. Again, the route is likely to be via your GP or other specialist local services.

Finally, for children with marked *attention problems* it may be recommended that your child sees a paediatrician, psychiatrist or clinical psychologist. The medically trained professionals – paedi-atrician and psychiatrist – will need to be involved if it is thought that your child might benefit from medication. Clinical psychol-ogists and child psychiatrists will give advice on family issues and practical management guidance for behavioural and attentional problems. The route is either through local Child and Adolescent Mental Health Services (CAMHS) or Child Development Clinics via school or the GP. School will advise you on the best referral route in your area.

For more information about what would be involved and what you might expect from an assessment from one of these professionals, see Chapter 8.

Jamie

Jamie was an eight year old boy whose parents and teachers were worried about his progress in reading and spelling, and with learning his times tables. He was also having difficulty concentrating and was becoming reluctant to do his homework. His parents completed our questionnaires and carried out the checks for dyslexia and dyscalculia.

After Jamie's parents talked through their concerns and the results of the questionnaires and checks, his teachers suggested a two-week period of watching and keeping track. After this time, it was clear that Jamie was indeed struggling and feeling both frustrated and miserable; it was decided that more was needed to help him. The next step was to involve the SENCO. The following week the SENCO observed Jamie in class, looked at his work books and did a reading and spelling test with him. As a result Jamie was put on School Action, and offered a Catch-up Programme. It was agreed to review his progress at the beginning of the following term.

When the review took place, Jamie had not made the hoped-for progress. A further Catch-up Programme was offered, but after another term it was clear that this was still insufficient as Jamie was continuing to fall behind. At the next review with the SENCO, it was decided to move Jamie to School Action Plus, and an IEP was prepared.

Jamie's IEP – School Action Plus

Chronological Age: 8 years 9 months
Reading Age: 7 years 0 months
Spelling Age: 6 years 3 months
Start Date: 8 January

Review Date: 8 July
Five times per week of 15-minute one-to-one sessions with Mrs Smith, LSA

Targets	Support	Success Strategies	Outcome Criteria by Date
To decode 2-, 3- & 4-letter words	Teaching in small steps using 2-, 3- & 4-letter nonsense words	Can decode 5 new nonsense words in a row correctly at each level	6 Feb – 2 letters 4 Mar – 3 letters 9 Apr – 4 letters

Targets	Support	Success Strategies	Outcome Criteria by Date
To learn 10 irregular words	Use SOS (say-cover-write then check/ repeat)	When able to spell all 10 correctly to dictation	10 Mar – 5 words 16 Apr – 10 words
To read short books willingly	Teacher supplies books to parents for home. Sticker for each page read. Give treat at end of book	When reading 2 books willingly/ week	10 Feb – 1 book 11 Mar – 2 books
To spell 3- & 4-letter words	Multisensory & phonic approach to building up _ed, _at, _in words. Parents back up with Word Lotto Game	When he spells 7 words of each type to dictation	9 Apr – 12 words learned
To learn tables	Step counting (e.g. 2, 4, 6...) Collect objects & group. Make a tables grid. Practise daily & reward	When he can say 2x, 5x & 10x tables correctly	12 Mar – 2x table 2 Apr – 5x table 2 May – 10x table
To work independently for 30 mins	Use timer set initially for 10 mins, then build up in 5-min steps & rewards	To complete set activity in 30 mins without distracting himself or others	2 Mar – 15 mins 9 Apr – 20 mins 6 May – 25 mins 9 Jun – 30 mins

Other agencies involved:

Jamie is on the waiting list to see the school's educational psychologist for assessment for possible dyslexia.*

If School Action Plus is not enough

Only for those with very severe difficulties, who are failing to make adequate progress on School Action Plus, will there be the possibility of moving on to a further stage of help. This process

* For the results of Jamie's assessment with the educational psychologist, see Chapter 8.

is known as '**statementing**' – meaning '**a Full Statutory Assessment leading to a Statement of Special Educational Needs**'. Statements aim to fund the child for around 10–20 hours of LSA support. In very rare instances, they may also allow for children to attend a special school or unit. Parents may request their child to be assessed for statementing, although it is usually initiated by the school. It is the LEA's decision whether or not to proceed with the statementing, though parents may appeal if a statement has been refused.

There are very strict **criteria** for statementing. The child's difficulties have to be so severe that he or she is in the bottom 1 per cent on a particular standardised test (mainly reading and/or IQ or a language measure). Children in the bottom 2 per cent may not qualify! A psychologist will need to carry out an assessment. Bear in mind that different LEAs may have slightly different criteria for statementing – and some educational psychologists working in schools do very little formal testing. The **decision** on statementing will be carried out by a panel of experts, which must include, as a minimum, a senior educational psychologist and a senior education officer from the Local (Education) Authority.

In recent times the number of statements has been greatly reduced, and they may eventually be phased out altogether. For example, in one Inner London primary school of 400 pupils, 20–25 per cent (around 100 children) are on the Special Needs Register but only eight have statements.

The routes by which school can help may seem complicated. The teachers are bound by what facilities and funds are available and have to make decisions about how these are distributed in their school. There have been quite a few changes in the procedures for supporting children with Special Educational Needs. Sometimes these changes occur every year; you will therefore need to check this out.

WHAT IS IMPORTANT ABOUT SPECIAL NEEDS TEACHING?

Special Needs needs special teaching

The usual teaching methods applied as part of Quality First Teaching may not work for children with specific learning difficulties. Children with special needs require more intensive teaching over and above Quality First Teaching. This means:

- giving more face-to-face teacher or LSA involvement in one-to-one or small groups
- 'differentiating' the child's curriculum: what is being taught is in keeping with the child's ability level, but may be at a much lower level than what is being taught to the rest of the class
- breaking down each learning task into small steps
- setting the size of the steps so that the child is able to experience a high level of success (so getting it right around 90 per cent of the time)
- giving lots of examples to show the child how to do each step
- providing lots of opportunity to *practise* so the new skills are frequently repeated and reinforced
- giving feedback to the child on progress, which needs to be *immediate*, *frequent*, very *clear* and coupled with *reward* for success (verbal praise, tick charts and so on)
- close teacher monitoring to check that the child is achieving the targets set before moving on
- good communication between LSA, SENCO and class teacher

The importance of specific teaching programmes

The content of teaching programmes for children with specific learning difficulties needs to be geared to their particular needs. Here are some guidelines.

Literacy difficulties

These have been shown to improve most with structured teaching programmes that emphasise phonological awareness training together with learning how to decode words. 'Sight word' learning of common irregular words like 'the' and 'was', together with reading whole books, is essential too. Some children may need additional help with their reading comprehension. Multisensory teaching (which encourages the child to use sight, hearing and movement from writing) reinforces all the sensory pathways to learning. There are many good structured phonic-based schemes that use a multisensory approach – for example Jolly Phonics, Phonographix, Toe by Toe. Individual schools will have their own preferences.

Dyspraxia/DCD/nonverbal learning difficulties

The problems at school for children with these difficulties are:

- illegible handwriting
- slow speed of work output
- poor presentation of work
- disorganisation
- inadequate study skills and exam techniques

Some severely affected children may be assessed by an occupational therapist or physiotherapist, whose assessment results and recommendations may be incorporated into the IEP. Generally, what will be offered is help with improving letter formation in handwriting, and starting cursive (joined-up) writing. Some children may be taught and encouraged to use computers for some of their written work – usually homework and projects but also for class work for those children with very severe difficulties.

Language difficulties

Many children who have problems in understanding and using spoken language will have seen a speech and language therapist when they were younger. A small number of older children might also get to see a speech therapist. He or she assesses what the child's particular problems are, for instance:

- understanding spoken language
- putting words together in the right order and in a grammatically correct way
- learning and remembering new words
- pronouncing speech sounds correctly

The speech therapist can suggest teaching strategies (which need to be written into the child's IEP) to help overcome these language problems. Psychologists at the University of York's Centre for Reading and Language have recently developed a special teaching programme for Reception class children who have poor speech and language. This is delivered by LSAs and the results are proving very promising. Not only was the children's language improved by this programme, but it also helped to pave the way to better classroom learning.

Maths problems
Teachers need to assess what problems a child is having with maths. For example, a particular child could have difficulties with:

- learning number bonds from 1–10
- understanding number sequences (for instance, odd numbers, 1, 3, 5 and so on)
- recognising and labelling shapes
- learning and remembering the basic operations of addition, subtraction, multiplication and division
- remembering multiplication tables

Once the problem areas have been identified, a programme can be set up to re-teach and thoroughly practise the relevant skills.

Attention problems
These affect all aspects of learning in the classroom. For children who need to learn to concentrate better and to not distract themselves and others, it will be important to set in place targets for the child to work towards in small, achievable

Accommodations

Children whose specific learning difficulties persist, despite extra help and support, may need **accommodations** in tests and examinations, including GCSEs and AS/A levels. An accommodation usually takes the form of extra time to complete written examination papers, but more severely affected children may be permitted a 'reader' (for the exam questions), a 'scribe' (to write down the answers) or a laptop computer.

Many children with specific learning difficulties are slow readers and/or writers. Others will have difficulties in finding their way around the examination paper and in processing and organising large amounts of information, especially under time pressure. Time accommodations greatly help these children.

Readers are provided only for those children who have very severe reading problems (for GCSEs the child would need to have a reading age level of under 10 years). Scribes may be provided for children with very severe spelling and/or motor control (and therefore handwriting) difficulties. Laptop computers are permitted only for children who have severe handwriting problems (either extreme slowness or poor legibility), and for whom typing has become their usual method of working.

These accommodations are arranged through the child's school. Professional assessments may need to be obtained to provide the evidence required for the accommodations requested. If it is extra time only that is wanted for GCSEs, an assessment by a psychologist or specialist teacher will need to be carried out at some time after Year 6. If the child requires a reader, scribe or use of a laptop, the assessment must have been done, at most, two years before the examination. A special form called an **Access for Special Examination Arrangements** is completed by the assessor and the school; this has to be on file for the examination boards to view *well* in advance of the examinations.

steps. Rewarding the child is key to success – for instance, using stickers or points (see Chapter 11 for ideas).

■ ■ ■

Your child's school will help you follow through concerns you may have about your child's learning. Or they may have already picked up on the problems and approached you. Either way the teachers are there to help. It's a partnership.

8

Taking Assessment Further

Your child's school – and you – may decide that a more in-depth assessment of your child's learning difficulties is needed. Such an assessment is likely to involve one or more of the specialists we mentioned in the previous chapter. Most often this is either a specialist teacher from the Local (Education) Authority or a psychologist. Sometimes other specialists may be involved too – most usually speech and language therapists or occupational therapists.

SEEING A PSYCHOLOGIST

A psychologist (who may be an educational psychologist or sometimes a clinical psychologist with a special interest in learning difficulties) is important for gaining an in-depth understanding of a child's learning needs. Standardised tests of learning are usually given so that the child's levels are compared with large numbers of children of the same age across the country. (Some educational psychologists prefer instead to look at the child's level of work compared with the rest of the class.) Psychologists use a very wide range of tests, some of which are 'closed' to other professionals (even specialist teachers). Of course, psychologists do not only look at test scores, but also try to understand the child as a whole; they will be watching carefully not just what the child does in a test but *how* it is done and what sort of mistakes are made.

The information from a psychologist's assessment is used to:

- give information about the child's type of learning problem
- understand the child's particular pattern of learning strengths and weaknesses
- help make decisions about what kind of support is needed
- give suggestions about what kind of teaching methods and materials would be suitable
- help decide what kind of school or learning environment might be best

What exactly do psychologists do?

If your child has been referred for an assessment, the psychologist will ask for detailed information from school and normally from you too. Sometimes questionnaires may be used to do this. Below, as an example, are our Teacher Questionnaire and Family Questionnaire. They will give you an idea of the kinds of information that will be needed. Reports from the SENCO, if one is already involved, IEPs and samples of the child's work will be requested. Educational psychologists working in schools may also see a child in the classroom.

Teacher Questionnaire (Confidential)

I have been given permission to contact you regarding _____.

I would be grateful if you could kindly complete the details and return the form to me at the above address by _____. Thank you very much for your co-operation.

Name of school . . . .

Year/form child is in . . . .

Number of children in class . . . .

Approximate position in class . . . .

Is child's attendance regular? . . . . YES/NO

Child's attainments in Basic Educational Subjects (relative to peers) – please tick as appropriate.

	Above Av.	Average	Below Av.	Well below Av.
Reading accuracy				
Reading comprehension				
Spelling				
Handwriting/presentation				
Written work				
Mathematics				

Is there provision at school for helping children with learning problems?   YES/NO
Is the child receiving this help?   YES/NO
If yes, please give details ....
....

Does the child have behavioural problems?   YES/NO
If yes, please give details ....
....

Does the child have social/peer relationship difficulties?   YES/NO
If yes, please give details ....
....

What is the child's attitude to school and to learning?
....
....

What is the child's attention and concentration like?
....
....

Any further comments?
....
....
....

Name (please print) _____ Date _____
Position:
Class Teacher, Headteacher, Special Needs Teacher, Other (please specify)

Family Questionnaire (Confidential)

Date of completion. . . . .

Child's full name. . . . .
Child's date of birth. . . . .   Age: . . . . . years . . . . . months . . . . .
Home address . . . .
. . . .
Telephone . . . .
Name and address of present school. . . . .
. . . .
Is it an independent or state school? . . . .
Name of present school headteacher . . . .

Please list names of other schools attended

Name	Type of school (i.e. nursery)	Age when child attended school	State or independent

. . . .
. . . .
Have I your permission to contact your child's school?   YES/NO

What is your child's attitude to school?
. . . .

What subjects does he/she find difficult at present?
. . . .

Please circle each of the following that is a particular problem now:
Reading / Reading Comprehension / Spelling / Handwriting / Written Work

At what age did his/her learning difficulties come to your attention and how?
. . . .
. . . .

Has your child had help from *outside* school?   YES/NO
If yes, what kind of help? How much? . . . .
. . . .

Has your child had help from school?   YES/NO
If yes, what kind of help? How much? . . . .
. . . .

Has your child had any other treatment (e.g. visits to specialists, speech centres)? YES/NO
If yes, please specify . . . .

Please give full details of date, address and name of psychologist who carried out any psychological assessment (and please forward a copy of the report if you are agreeable)
. . . .
. . . .

DEVELOPMENT AND HEALTH
Has your child had any problems with physical health, including eyesight and hearing?
If yes, give details. . . . .

Were there any problems with the birth? . . . .
. . . .

At what age was your child walking without help? . . . .

At what age was your child beginning to say a few words? . . . .

Do you think your child's early language development was generally early/average/late?. . . . .

Have you noticed your child having any difficulties in talking or communicating?. . . . .

Is English the only language spoken at home? YES/NO
If no, please specify . . . .

Does your child have difficulty in concentrating on school work?
. . . .

Does your child have difficulty in remembering instructions?
. . . .

Is your child left- or right-handed? . . . .

Is your child well co-ordinated? Please describe any difficulties
. . . .

BEHAVIOURAL, SOCIAL OR EMOTIONAL ADJUSTMENT
Has your child had any problems with behaviour at home or school? How
well does he/she get on with other children? Are there any emotional
concerns such as fears, anxiety and so on? Please describe

....
....
....
....

Are there any special family circumstances that could have affected your
child's development and progress (e.g. divorce, bereavement)?

....
....
....
....

Have other members of the family (including both parents' families) had
learning, reading, spelling or language difficulties? If so, please state family
member and nature of difficulty

....
....
....
....

Child's difficulties. Please describe in detail (continuing over page if
necessary) your concerns and the difficulties shown by your child. Include a
brief history if possible

....
....
....
....
....
....
....
....
....

Signed .... Date..............
Relationship to child..

THE TESTS PSYCHOLOGISTS USE

A range of tests will be given at an assessment to get the full picture of your child's problems. These will vary according to the difficulties your child has, and the questions that you and the teachers are asking. Individual psychologists will also have preferences for some tests over others. Typical tests given would include ability tests, educational attainment tests, and tests of specific skills such as memory, phonological awareness and attention. It is worth looking at these in some detail to help you understand the report that the psychologist prepares about your child.

Tests of ability/intelligence

Some people get really upset about the idea of intelligence testing because they think their child will be labelled in a negative way and that the information might be used against him or her. It is sometimes felt that intelligence tests don't measure really important aspects of a person such as social and emotional skills, sense of humour and artistic or musical creativity. And of course such thinking is right! But in practice a comprehensive ability/IQ test is very helpful for understanding how children learn and why they might not be progressing at school.

The most used IQ tests do not provide just a single figure as a measure of ability but have at least two (and usually more) scores. For instance, the IQ test most commonly used by psychologists is the WISC (Wechsler Intelligence Scales for Children). This has two main IQ figures, currently called index scores (IQ and index scores mean the same thing): a verbal comprehension index (or verbal IQ) and a perceptual reasoning index (or nonverbal IQ). The verbal index or IQ is a measure of *spoken language ability*; the score shows how the child performed on tests of vocabulary and verbal reasoning. The nonverbal index or IQ is a measure of *visual-spatial ability*; here the score shows how the child performed on puzzle- and pattern-based tests. The two IQ scores may be combined to give an overall indication of ability, called general or full scale IQ.

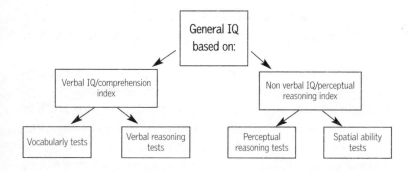

The WISC has two more scales that give index scores: the processing speed index and the working memory index. The processing speed index shows how the child performed on two paper-and-pencil tasks that test how quickly children can process and respond to visual information. The working memory index shows how a child did on tests of remembering and repeating back strings of numbers and letters. Many children with written language difficulties or with dyspraxia will have slow speeds on the processing speed tests. Many children with dyslexia, dyscalculia or language problems will have working memory difficulties.

The information that the IQ scores give can be used to do the following:

Give an accurate picture of what can be expected from the child educationally: Estimates of ability by teachers and parents (who may not have much opportunity to compare an individual child with the wider population of children of the same age) can be way off the mark. Getting children's ability levels wrong can have serious consequences for how they are seen and taught and how they see themselves.

Separate out types of learning difficulty: IQ scores are based on a nationwide average of 100. Children whose IQ levels are around the 100 mark have average ability and would, therefore, be expected to achieve educationally at around the middle of their class (though a child with an average IQ will be below the *class average* in a very high-ability class – or indeed above the class average in a low-ability class). Children who have high IQs – say 120+ – would be expected to be very competent educationally. Children with average or above-average IQs who are struggling education-ally and often described by parents and teachers as 'not fulfilling their potential' may well have a specific learning difficulty.

Children who score rather low on IQ tests (below 80) will struggle in learning compared with their classmates; these chil-dren are described as having *general learning difficulties*. Before they are tested, the extent of their learning difficulties may not be so obvious, especially if the child gets along well socially. Good, consistent teaching and lots of repetition that follows the child's own pace of learning is important. Such children may need to follow a curriculum within the classroom different from that of their peers (the 'differentiated curriculum').

Understand the impact of patterns of ability on learning: The pattern of the IQ scores makes a big difference. Expectations of high learning achievement are based largely on the verbal IQ; this is the IQ figure that has the closest 'predictive' relationship with educational performance. However, children with good nonverbal abilities who do not have such good verbal abilities may show a talent for art, technical skills and visual creativity, even if their academic performance is not strong. Psychologists look at whether or not there is a difference between the verbal and nonverbal IQs, and how big this difference is. Children who seem bright and have a good verbal IQ but who are struggling in school may, before testing, have been labelled as 'careless' and 'lazy'. If, after testing, a low nonverbal IQ is revealed, the child may then be recognised as having dyspraxia or nonverbal learn-ing difficulties. Children with the opposite pattern (high nonverbal IQ but low verbal IQ) may have been seen as gener-ally slow learners but, after testing, have been shown to have a specific language difficulty.

Tests of educational skills

Tests of educational attainment cover skills taught in the class-room: reading, spelling, written work and maths. It is usually important for the psychologist to look at all of these, even if you or the teachers think that there is a problem in only one area. It is useful to know how children cope with each skill, and what the pattern of their strengths and weaknesses is. As we have said before, having one educational difficulty often goes hand in hand with other problems too. For instance, many children with dyslexia not only have reading and spelling problems but have difficulties in maths also.

Testing reading

Reading involves a number of different skills, each of which needs to be assessed separately:

- Single word reading tests assess the size of the child's *reading vocabulary*.
- Reading sentences or passages assesses how well *context* is used to help read words.
- The child's approach to reading, sometimes called *word attack*, can be looked at too; for example, does the child sound out every letter in a word, guess at what it says using the context or skip unknown words?
- Reading passages also allows the psychologist to measure the child's *speed* and *fluency* of reading.
- *Reading comprehension* is often assessed by asking the child to answer detailed questions about the content of the passage or sentence.
- Tests of nonsense (or non-word) reading, similar to those described in the checks of Chapter 1, assess the child's ability to *decode* or sound out unfamiliar words using their

Types of Reading Tests

- Single word reading
- Prose reading
- Reading comprehension
- Reading speed and fluency
- Non-word reading

knowledge of sound-to-letter rules. Children with dyslexia typically show a pattern in which their ability to read real words is very much better than their ability to read nonsense words. This is because their main problem is learning to decode.

Testing spelling

Spelling skills are usually assessed by asking children to write down single words, some regular and some irregular. This gives the psychologist a good idea of the size of the child's spelling vocabulary and how it relates to other children of the same age. It is also useful to know whether the type of mistake made is *phonetic* or *non-phonetic*. A phonetic mistake means that the child spells the word incorrectly, but the letters of each sound are still present in the spelling – for instance, spelling 'right' as 'rite', 'whistle' as 'wisel' and 'done' as 'dun'. A non-phonetic mistake means that the attempted spelling when read out loud does not sound like the intended word. Examples of non-phonetic mistakes include spelling 'climb' as 'chiy', 'hand' as 'nady', 'counting' as 'caty'. These sorts of mistakes make it very hard for the reader to follow what is written.

Testing writing skills

Psychologists will want to see what the child's *handwriting* looks like. For younger children, judgements about *letter formation* and *legibility* will be the main concerns. For older children (who sit written tests and exams), *speed* of writing is important too. Creative writing can be assessed by asking children to write a passage of their own, usually on a set topic; it is important to look at their ability to sequence a story, organise it into paragraphs, produce full sentences without making grammatical mistakes, and spell and punctuate accurately.

Testing maths

Tests of maths usually concentrate on mental arithmetic and curriculum knowledge. Curriculum knowledge can be separated into, first, knowledge of the basic numerical operations of addition, subtraction, multiplication and division; and second, mathematics reasoning, which covers a broader range of concepts and principles and also looks at problem-solving ability.

Types of Maths Tests

■ Mental arithmetic
■ Numerical operations (written calculations)
■ Mathematical reasoning

Tests of specific learning difficulties

These are sometimes called 'diagnostic tests' because they help the psychologist look beneath the surface at what underlying learning difficulties might be causing the child's underperformance at school.

Testing for dyslexia

There are four sets of tests that many psychologists regard as 'dyslexia sensitive'. First, *nonsense word reading* (see Chapter 1). Difficulties with nonsense word reading show up the decoding problems typical of children with dyslexia. Other important dyslexia-sensitive tests are the phonological abilities tests, in particular measures of *phonological awareness*. You will already be familiar with what makes up a phonological awareness test from the checks you made in Chapter 1 (the 'take away a sound' and the 'saying words backwards' tests). Phonological skill can also be assessed using *naming speed* tests; for instance, asking children to name rows of pictures, randomly ordered letters or numbers as fast as they can. Finally, many children with dyslexia have *short-term verbal working memory* difficulties. These are usually assessed with a digit span test that involves the child repeating strings of random numbers of increasing length, both forwards and then backwards – and sometimes also with a test of nonsense word repetition (as you did for the check items in Chapter 1).

Types of Dyslexia-sensitive Tests

- Decoding (non-word reading)
- Phonological awareness
- Phonological processing (rapid naming)
- Short-term verbal memory (digit span)

Testing for dyspraxia

Children described as having dyspraxia will often obtain much lower nonverbal than verbal IQ scores. The psychologist may, however, want to give further tests that are sensitive to the perceptual, spatial and motor problems typical of these children. The tests could include copy drawing, measures of eye-hand co-ordination and pencil control under timed conditions, jigsaw puzzle-style tasks and assessment of memory for visual patterns. If the child's problem looks to be particularly severe, and a special programme might be needed, then a referral to an occupational therapist or physiotherapist for further assessment could be suggested.

Testing for underlying maths problems

Seeing how the child manages tests of mental arithmetic and curriculum-based mathematics is just the first step in deciding whether the problem might be dyscalculia. It is also important to assess the underlying learning difficulties causing the problems with maths. This might include maths marker tests of the kind used in checks in Chapter 5. Sometimes, children with dyscalculia have nonverbal (in particular spatial and visual perceptual) difficulties that make it hard for them to grasp visual concepts within maths – like setting out sums on a page, understanding fractions, knowing where to place decimal points, understanding geometry and symmetry and so on. Other children who have maths problems could have verbal working memory difficulties that make it hard for them to do mental arithmetic – they can't 'hold on to' numbers in their short-term memory while carrying out calculations with them. Some of the tests used for assessing dyspraxia, together with a digit span test, are helpful for looking at underlying problems in maths.

Testing for language problems

Children with speech and language difficulties that persist into the school years will usually have a low verbal IQ (but a relatively normal nonverbal IQ). Language is very complex and is made up of a number of different skills, only some of which are assessed by a verbal IQ test. The psychologist may explore further by giving language marker tests – including tests of verbal memory used in the checks in Chapters 1 and 3 (repeating nonsense words and long sentences). The psychologist may go on to give tests of verbal understanding – of words and of sentences. If the child's language difficulties look to be particularly problematical, referral to a speech and language therapist is recommended; a more 'fine grained' assessment will enable the therapist to say whether the child would benefit from speech and language therapy.

Testing for attention problems

This is not such an easy area to assess, though some psychologists are now beginning to make use of standardised tests. Making a diagnosis of attention deficit (with or without hyperactivity) disorder can be complex. Many professionals feel that it should be made by a multidisciplinary team of not just psychologists and teachers, but also paediatricians or psychiatrists. There are questionnaires for parents and teachers to rate children's concentration and the other behaviours that may accompany an attention deficit disorder. Psychologists who work in schools may carry out a discreet 'fly on the wall' observation in the classroom of whether the child can stay on task, not get distracted, not fidget or cause a disturbance to other children. If it is thought that medication should be considered, children with severe attention problems must be referred to a medical doctor (psychiatrist or paediatrician).

The psychologist's report

Once the testing is done, the psychologist writes a report for you and the teachers. Of course, the way this looks depends on the style of the individual psychologist, but there are key areas that you should expect to find covered:

- why the referral was made in the first place
- a description of the concerns and views of parents and teachers
- a summary of the test results
- a description of the child's behaviour during testing
- a statement of what the psychologist thinks the problem is – what some would call a 'formulation' or 'diagnosis' – including whether or not there are any co-occurring difficulties

The report should also provide suggestions of what to do. These would include:

- whether or not the child needs extra help
- how often help should be given
- what form the help should take (individual or small group, given by the SENCO or learning support assistant or by an outside school specialist teacher)
- what teaching methods might be used (for example, multisensory learning or a structured phonic programme)
- how to help the child use strengths in learning to compensate for difficulties
- how parents can help and support at home
- how to keep up children's motivation to learn, general confidence and self-esteem
- whether other professionals should be involved
- whether the child needs 'accommodations', such as extra time or using laptops in exams
- what might be expected of the child's progress in the short and longer term
- when the child's progress should be reviewed

After the assessment you should try to talk through the results with both the psychologist and teachers. Keeping in touch with the psychologist and the school will make it easier to follow up your child's progress.

Jamie's Psychological Assessment

Jamie, the eight year old introduced in Chapter 7, has had his psychological assessment. The test results are given below. If you are unfamiliar with some of the technical terms then do look at the box on page 150.

Ability Tests

WECHSLER INTELLIGENCE SCALE FOR CHILDREN IV (WISC-IV)

Verbal Comprehension Index *(Verbal IQ) = 102*		*Perceptual Reasoning Index* *(Nonverbal IQ) = 94*	
Similarities	11	Block Design	7
Vocabulary	10	Matrix Reasoning	10
Comprehension	11	Picture Completion	10

Processing Speed Index = 91		*Working Memory Index = 88*	
Coding	8	Digit Span	7
Symbol Search	9	Letter-number Sequencing	9

(Average score for all these subtests – at any age – is 10)

Attainment Tests

READING
Wechsler Individual Achievement Test (WIAT) Single Word Reading Test:

Standard Score = 85
Percentile 16
Age Equivalent 7y 0m

Neale Analysis of Reading Ability (NARA) Prose Reading Test:

Accuracy   Standard Score = 90
Percentile 26
Age Equivalent 7y 7m

Comprehension	Standard Score = 96
	Percentile 40
	Age Equivalent 8y 7m

WIAT Pseudoword Decoding: Standard Score = 76
                             Percentile 5
                             Age Equivalent 5y 8m

SPELLING
WIAT Spelling Test: Standard Score = 78
                             Percentile 7
                             Age Equivalent 6y 8m

HANDWRITING
Poorly formed letters, printing only, occasionally writes letters back to front.

MATHS
WIAT Numerical Operations: Standard Score = 90
                              Percentile 32
                              Age Equivalent 8y 0m

WIAT Mathematics Reasoning: Standard Score = 98
                              Percentile 45
                              Age Equivalent 8y 0m

Diagnostic Tests

SHORT-TERM MEMORY TESTS
Auditory/Verbal Memory (WISC-IV Digit Span): weak overall, but especially poor at digits backwards.

Visual Memory (Children's Memory Scales Dot Locations):
                              Scaled Score = 8

PHONOLOGICAL PROCESSING
Comprehensive Test of Phonological Processing (CTOPP):
    Phonological Awareness: Elision Scaled Score = 6
                              Blending Words Scaled Score = 7
                              Composite Score 79

    Rapid Naming   Digit Naming Scaled Score = 8
                              Letter Naming Scaled Score = 7
                              Composite Score 85

FINE MOTOR CO-ORDINATION AND MOTOR ORGANISATION
Rey Complex Figure Copy Drawing   Percentile: In lowest 10%

These test results show that Jamie is of average intelligence. His maths skills are developing as expected for his age and ability, but he is underachieving in reading, writing and spelling. The diagnostic tests show that he has underlying phonological processing and short-term memory difficulties typical of children with dyslexia. There are some additional (co-occurring) visual-spatial and fine motor problems that are seen in children with dyspraxia.

Understanding Test Results

When any test is developed it is first given to a large number of children. This creates a *standardisation* sample against which an individual child's score can be compared. This means that children's ability level or progress can be assessed more accurately than by simply comparing them with classmates.

In a psychological report scores may be described in one of four ways:

1. *Raw scores* – these are the number of items a child gets correct (for example, the total number of words read). The trouble with this type of score is that it is hard to see how well a child has done because different tests vary in length and difficulty.

2. *Standard and scaled scores* – these are most often used by psychologists, especially for IQ and educational attainment tests (reading, spelling and maths). With these you can see where a child's level is in relation to the average across the country for others of the same age.

Scaled scores have a mean or average of 10 (and are usually used for subtests that form part of a larger test – for instance, the WISC-IV).

Standard scores have a mean or average of 100 and are used for IQ and many reading, spelling and maths tests.

A child's score falls within the average range if it is between 9 and 11 for scaled scores and between 90 and 110 for standard scores. Scaled scores of above 11 and standard scores of above 110 mean that a child is above average in that skill. The opposite is also true: scaled scores below 9 and standard scores below 90 show that a child is having some difficulty with that skill.

3. *Percentiles (or centiles or percentile ranks)* – these show the percentage of the standardisation sample that has scored *at* or *below* that particular score. So, if a child obtains a percentile of 80, this means that 80 per cent of children of that age in the standardisation sample scored at or below that child's level; the child therefore has done very well indeed and is in the top 20 per cent. A percentile score of 10 means that only 10 per cent of the standardisation sample scored below this child's level. The child can therefore be seen to be in the bottom 10 per cent on that test.

4. *Age equivalent scores* – an age equivalent score gives an approximate level in years and months of a child's level on a particular test. Unfortunately, although age equivalents seem easy to understand, they do not allow a comparison of children's performance across different ages or across different tests. This is because the 'spread' (or range) of scores around the mean may vary according to age and the particular test used. For example, if a child's score was six and a half years on a reading test and seven and a half years on a maths test, it would not necessarily mean that a child's maths was a full year ahead of his or her reading. It is best, therefore, to use age equivalent scores alongside standard scores and/or percentiles.

Scaled scores, standard scores and percentiles have an important advantage over age equivalents because they allow comparisons across different tests and at different ages. So a child with a standard score of 110 on a reading test but a standard score of 90 on a maths test would show clearly that he or she is a good reader but relatively weak in maths. Standard scores can also show whether or not children are improving – or getting worse – as they get older. So a child who has a reading standard score of 75 at age seven, but a reading standard score of 90 at age nine, has made a great improvement. The score has gone up from being well below average to within the lower end of the average range. But if the standard score goes down, then progress can be seen to be slow.

SEEING A SPEECH AND LANGUAGE THERAPIST

If a child has a particular problem with language or communication, you, the school or the psychologist might feel that a more detailed assessment would be helpful. Speech and language therapists are usually part of the health service system and are based in clinics or hospitals. Children would therefore need to be referred by the GP or a paediatrician if they are not already being seen in a hospital department. Some speech and language therapists will see children privately too (see Organisations and Resources on page 227 for contact details).

The speech and language therapist will first carry out an assessment using standardised tests for the following separate skills (also summarised in the diagram below):

- receptive language (the child's understanding of what is said)
- expressive language (the child's ability to communicate thoughts in spoken words)
- articulation (how clearly the child speaks and is understood by others)

Expressive language can be further divided into:

- phonology (the child's ability to process and produce the speech sounds accurately)
- semantics (the meaning of language – mainly refers to vocabulary knowledge)
- grammar (saying words in the right order within a sentence and using correct parts of speech, like tenses)
- pragmatics (the use of language socially)

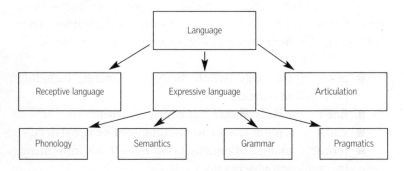

After the assessment, the therapist can then decide whether speech and language therapy would help. The therapy may be given in a block of weekly sessions, say over six weeks with follow-ups to monitor progress. Children with more severe difficulties may be offered weekly or fortnightly therapy over a longer period of time. Also, advice is usually given to teachers and parents about what they can do to help improve the child's communication at school and at home.

SEEING A PAEDIATRICIAN OR PSYCHIATRIST

Both paediatricians and child psychiatrists are medical doctors. Paediatricians specialise in children's physical health and development. Psychiatrists are specialists in mental health. Other professionals, in particular psychologists and speech and language therapists, usually have a greater involvement in children's learning difficulties than medical doctors. However, children might be referred to a paediatrician if there is a problem with hearing or vision or if some medical syndrome is suspected. A psychiatrist could become involved for children who have severe ADHD and for whom medication is being considered.

SEEING A PHYSICAL THERAPIST (OCCUPATIONAL THERAPIST OR PHYSIOTHERAPIST)

Occupational therapists (OTs) and physiotherapists assess physical skills and are therefore often asked to see children who have co-ordination problems or nonverbal learning difficulties. They will use standardised tests and observations to look at:

- gross motor skills (whole body movements, including posture and balance)
- fine motor skills (finger and pencil control)
- visual perception (ability to discriminate fine visual details)
- motor planning and organisational skills (body movements in an integrated sequence)
- sensory integration (the ability to put together information from different senses – such as co-ordinating hand movements with vision i.e. visual-motor integration)
- body awareness

Following the assessment, the OT or physiotherapist may take a child on for a planned block of therapy. Exercises to strengthen muscle groups or to develop sensory skills are likely to be suggested for home as well.

■ ■ ■

You now have an overview of what can be achieved from an assessment by professionals who specialise in children's learning difficulties. Psychologists, speech and language therapists and physical therapists assess a wide range of learning, language, physical and educational problems. Discussions with the professionals, and the written report that follows, will give you a full picture of your child's potential and how this relates to current attainment. It will help you understand what specific learning difficulties your child has – and what needs to be done to help.

9

Alternative Therapies

Earlier in this book we talked about the three ways of looking at learning difficulties – biological, cognitive and behavioural (see page 110). Most therapies for specific learning difficulties work at the cognitive and behavioural levels. For instance, teachers of children with dyslexia usually train phonological awareness (cognitive level) and decoding, reading and spelling skills (behavioural level). These methods are tried and tested, and a great deal of scientific research has shown that they do improve the literacy skills of children with dyslexia.

Much new research is being done into the biological causes of specific learning difficulties; scientists are looking for the genes for dyslexia and are trying to locate the parts of the brain that might be affected in children with dyslexia. Understanding which genes are faulty may prove useful for gene therapy in the future. Alongside this research has come a range of 'alternative' therapies that claim to 'cure' learning difficulties by treating their biological cause – but not by doing any work directly on reading (or other educational skills).

SOME COMMON ALTERNATIVE THERAPIES

Monocular occlusion

This therapy involves children wearing special spectacles so that they can see with only one eye. This is supposed to help integrate information from both eyes and so stop words from looking blurred or jumping about. Some studies have suggested that this might indeed be useful for a small number of children with reading difficulties. However, it is hard to know from these whether improvements in reading are due to the spectacles or to other teaching the child is receiving at the same time.

Coloured overlays or tinted lenses

Started by Helen Irlen, who suggested that some poor readers suffer from 'scotopic sensitivity' (uncomfortable glare and distortion effects when seeing black print on white paper), this therapy involves wearing special spectacles or placing transparent coloured overlays on top of the text the child is reading. Looking at the evidence, tinted lenses or overlays may well help to make reading a more comfortable experience for a small number of children who then become more motivated to read – but it should not be seen as a replacement for systematic teaching of reading.

Primitive reflex therapy (and related 'brushing' therapy)

Children are either taught movement sequences or are stroked with a paintbrush, the aim being to reduce (and even eliminate) persisting primitive reflexes that should have stopped at an early age – for example, neck jerking reflexes. There has been a published study showing improvements in reading following reflex therapy. However, since the amount of 'exercising' the children did and what other reading instruction was given at the same time were not 'controlled', it is hard to be sure whether it was the therapy that was leading to the reading improvements. Having primitive reflexes that do not drop out could be a marker of an immature neurological system in a child with learning difficulties. These reflexes may, however, be unrelated to the skills needed for reading and writing, so the physical exercises might well make the reflexes disappear but with no effect at all on reading.

Dore method (or DDAT)

This method involves motor exercises aimed at improving the function of the cerebellum (the back part of the brain concerned with movement, balance, eye-tracking and so on). The treatment takes a long time (up to a year). There are some published studies about the effectiveness of the Dore method, but these have been heavily criticised by many academics and professionals.

Essential fatty acids/fish oil supplements

This treatment is based on the theory that children with learning difficulties are not able to easily metabolise essential fatty acids from their diet. They are then given (fairly large) doses of fish oils as a dietary supplement. There is some evidence that fish oils may help children with mild attention problems, but whether reading can be helped is far less clear. Studies have also warned that large doses of fish oil can have some harmful effects on health.

DO ALTERNATIVE THERAPIES LIVE UP TO THEIR CLAIMS?

Alternative therapies can look very attractive. They are seductive because they appear scientifically based and also seem to offer a quick fix. Some parents feel desperate because their child's progress seems too slow and they want to make sure they have tried everything and anything that just might help. It is worth remembering, though, that the research into the biological causes of learning difficulties is still at a very early stage. Most scientists, including psychologists, feel that the knowledge base and evidence for the effectiveness of biological therapies is not sufficient to recommend them. And remember that almost any treatment you feel you can believe in is going to lead to some kinds of improvements or other benefits (see below).

So, if you are tempted to try an alternative therapy, first ask yourself the following questions.

What's the evidence?

Many organisations offering alternative therapies provide only anecdotal evidence that their treatment works, that is, they rely on testimonials from parents who say their child improved as a result of the therapy. This is not the same thing as evidence that a treatment really works. What is needed is a scientific study (preferably more than one study) clearly showing that a group of children with a particular learning difficulty improved in their educational skills after treatment *when compared with a group of children with the same kind and level of difficulty who did not have the treatment.*

Does the treatment claim to cure 'everything'?

Does the treatment claim to cure not just dyslexia but also dyspraxia, ADHD, autism and lots more besides? Bear in mind that it is most unlikely that one particular treatment could be used for *all* learning difficulties.

Does the treatment lead to educational improvements – or something else?

Many testimonials by parents whose children have received alternative therapies concentrate on how much their child's confidence has increased, but not always on whether their reading, for instance, has improved. If a therapy claims to cure dyslexia, it should improve children's reading and spelling, not just their confidence. Any approach that gives children attention and support is likely to make them feel happier and more confident, even if their reading skills stay the same.

Is the treatment good value for money?

Fish oils to help your child improve concentration are relatively cheap (and even if they don't 'cure' the learning problems, at least they are thought to have some health benefits). But any expensively advertised programme with lots of glossy packaging could end up costing you thousands of pounds with no guarantee of improvement in your child's learning difficulty.

■ ■ ■

The overall message is *be cautious*. Of course, you want to help your child in every way you can. As parents, you may be understandably worried if your child is not improving as fast as you expected after following a systematic teaching programme. But don't give up on these programmes – they are backed by good scientific evidence, they work directly on the child's learning and educational difficulties, and they do offer good value for money. Be patient – sometimes things can take a little longer than you would want, especially for a child who has quite complex problems. If you do have money available to spend to help with your child's learning difficulty, we strongly advise you to go for one-to-one teaching with an appropriately qualified specialist teacher (check out specialist organisations such as BDA, Dyslexia Action and PATOSS, see Organisations and Resources on page 227).

Helping Your Child at Home

School can, and will, do much to help your child deal with a recognised specific learning difficulty (or several difficulties). But you – the parents – have a unique and crucial role to play. You know your child better than anyone else does. You have the advantage of being a permanent fixture in your child's life, whereas teachers usually change annually in the primary school years, and several teachers are involved in secondary school. Your job may be a hard one, but you can make a big difference to how your child copes with a learning difficulty.

You may already have approached school, and your child may be receiving help. Step One was about following up your concerns about your child by getting a better understanding of what his or her problems might be. Step Two was to approach school and develop a partnership with the teachers, and to link in with appropriate professionals for further assessment if needed. Step Three – the focus of the next two chapters – is what you can do at home. Chapter 10 covers what *you* can do to help your child develop the specific skills of reading, spelling, writing, maths and language. Chapter 11 looks at how you can help your child develop his or her attention, organisation and study skills.

Helping your child at home should be viewed as positive action. You and your child are partners in promoting learning skills and coping mechanisms – not just serving to 'patch up' failures. Your attitude towards your child's learning difficulties and the help you give at home can have a psychologically important effect on his or her attitude too. Your child will feel more motivated and self-confident if he or she stops feeling a failure but can think instead in terms of moving forward successfully.

COPING WITH THE IMPACT ON THE FAMILY

Having a child with a learning difficulty is bound to cause worries and stresses for parents in particular, but also for other family members. Knowing that your child has a difficulty is stressful. Parents quite reasonably worry how their children are going to cope with school now – and later with public exams, with qualifications and job prospects, and with life in general. But understanding the nature of the difficulty will lead to *less* stress all round. If you don't know what the problem is you may feel helpless. If you know what the problem is (even if it is a severe one) and have some ideas about how to help, you feel empowered and can see a way ahead.

Spot the causes of stress

To help you cope with the effect on the wider family of having a child with a learning difficulty, it is worth understanding the ways in which stresses can come about. The child with a learning difficulty – even before it's recognised – may well have taken up a lot more of your time and attention. For example, you may need to go up to school more often to sort out problems with teachers, or spend more time with your child on homework, learning spelling lists or looking for lost things, and so on. If one child is receiving more of your time and attention, it follows that any brothers and sisters might get less – they could feel left out or less special.

Competition between brothers and sisters can easily be made worse when one has learning difficulties. The problems can be expressed in different ways, depending on the level of ability and the personality of the other children and their age in relation to the child. More able and confident younger children may soon be yapping at the heels of – even overtaking – the child with a learning difficulty. This can create emotional havoc for the older child, and leave parents with the challenge of supporting the older child while at the same time encouraging the development and progress of the younger. On the other hand, if it is a younger child who has a learning difficulty, he or she may well feel badly in comparison to the 'perfect' successful

older one. This can often lead to the child with learning difficulties giving up or rebelling.

Parents can feel, even if they don't want to admit it, disap-
pointed that their child is not doing as well as they had hoped or
expected. Most parents have very strong desires and natural wishes
for their children to do well in school (and life). Unfortunately, the
child with a learning difficulty often ends up feeling a failure for
not meeting his or her parents' hopes and expectations. This
happens even when parents bend over backwards to reassure the
child that he or she is doing fine, and that the main thing to do is
to try hard and do his or her best. It happens even when parents
reassure the child that *all* their children are loved equally and have
different special talents and needs.

There may be a history of the child's learning difficulties not
being recognised and the child instead being seen as 'lazy', 'difficult' and 'obstinate'. Children who feel criticised are more likely
to develop a pattern of poor motivation, a tendency to avoid
work and even problems with behaviour. Stress can also occur
when parents worry about other children picking on or bullying
their struggling child; the child with low self-esteem is especially
vulnerable.

Many families experience a wide range of worries, not just
having a child with a learning difficulty. Parents may have their
own relationship problems; there may be a family member who
is ill or has a chronic health problem; there may be financial or
job concerns; or brothers and sisters may have their own issues
that demand time and attention. When parents are preoccupied,
it is more likely that one child's learning difficulties, especially if
these are mild, will go undetected for longer.

Ways to cut the stress

Once your child's difficulties are understood, that alone should
help you feel better. Recognising the possible sources of stress
within the wider family will enable everybody to act differently
and hopefully reduce stress too. Talk to your child with the
learning difficulty about the problems he or she has. Help your
child understand that the difficulties are not his or her fault

(that's how your child was born and there are many other children like him or her). Explain, if there is a family history of learning problems, that this is where your child's come from; and that having a learning difficulty does not mean he or she is stupid and won't do well in school and later on in life.

Feed back the results of the assessments from teachers and psychologists to your child in a form that he or she can easily understand. For younger children, start by saying how well he or she coped with testing, and explain all the things he or she was good at. Say that some things were not so good (some of which your child already knows, so you are just confirming it). For example, for a child with dyslexia, you might say, 'You were really good at answering the questions and your maths is fine – but you know how you find spelling difficult and that's what was found in the tests. The reason the spelling is hard for you is that you find it difficult to build up sounds in words.' For older children, you will want to give more explanation, but it's not usually a good idea to give details of scores as they are easily misinterpreted. It's fine to say if your child is in the top 10 per cent for, say, maths or at his or her age level (average). But it would be demoralising to tell your child he or she is in the bottom 5 per cent for spelling – there are kinder ways of saying it.

Talk to your child, perhaps together with a teacher too, about the kind of extra help that will be needed to get round his or her difficulties. For example, for the younger child with dyslexia, explain that the special teacher will help him or her to learn about sounds and how to build these up to make words so that your child learns to both read and spell more easily. For the older child, explain how you and your child can work together at home too to improve his or her spelling, writing and how to study and do exams.

Discuss any other worries your child might have – such as being picked on by other children – so that you can be supportive and reassuring. You should then talk to the teachers to make sure this stops. The teachers will also need to talk to the other children in the class about how to be understanding and helpful to children with learning or other difficulties.

Talk, preferably with your child's agreement, to other members of the family (brothers and sisters but also grandparents) about your child's learning difficulties and the need for extra help. That way, older children can be more understanding and maybe help out in some practical ways too. Younger children, who (from the viewpoint of the child with learning difficulties) are a pest, can perhaps be prevented from provoking or annoying the older one by means of their own reward chart (rewards for being nice and kind and for leaving the older sibling alone while he or she's doing homework or with friends).

Don't take all the stress yourself. Some parents are very good at covering up their anxieties about their children and can work well with them. If this is too hard for you, maybe another family member or close friend can help you out with some of the exercises and action plans we suggest. Join associations such as the British Dyslexia Association (BDA), Dyslexia Action, the Dyspraxia Foundation, the ADHD UK Alliance, AFASIC (Association for all Speech Impaired Children) (see Organisations and Resources on page 227). Most of these organisations host local events so you can meet other families who have children with similar difficulties. This is a really good way of getting support and practical advice.

■ ■ ■

Now you have talked through with your child – and with the rest of the family – the 'business' of the learning problem, you are ready to start working together. What you do with your child at home can promote many different skills, often several at the same time. For example, just hearing your child read helps to promote reading vocabulary, language development, concentration, enjoyment of books and confidence in reading out loud.

The strategies and techniques discussed are largely directed towards children who have a marked specific learning difficulty (or difficulties). But the actions suggested are also beneficial for children with milder problems. Our suggestions are based on approaches known to promote children's learning in an encouraging and non-threatening way.

10

Working on Reading, Writing, Language and Maths

WHAT YOU CAN DO: READING

Read with your child at home

For **children of seven to eight**, whose reading has scarcely got off the ground, it is crucial that parents read aloud *to* them *every day*. This will help your child to:

- realise and understand that books tell fantastic stories and are the source of interesting information (it is this that encourages children to *want* to read)
- become familiar with the 'concepts of print' (from looking at books children learn how they are constructed and organised, and that print is not something to be frightened of)
- become good at *listening* comprehension (if children can understand and remember what they hear, it will make *reading* comprehension easier later on)
- feel that reading is a routine part of everyday life – not a chore, just something that everybody does (this encourages reading as a good habit)
- learn (if needed) and practise using and seeing alphabet letters (if your child is still struggling with even a few alphabet letters, it will be worth going back to some alphabet story books; this might seem a bit babyish, but even many older children like to go back to easy, old favourites) – and you can even put an alphabet frieze on the wall as a regular reminder

For **older children** with dyslexia, who have made a start with reading but who are still struggling, you need to do 'shared reading' together at home. When you read together, you take turns in being the reader and the listener. This takes pressure off the child who is 'rewarded' for a bit of effort by relaxing while the parent reads. (Children still have to listen and take in what is read, but the story can move along more quickly, and so be more interesting and enjoyable.)

Tips for success with shared reading

■ Make the reading sessions (almost) daily and short (10 minutes is fine).

■ Curl up in a quiet and comfy place – and not at the very moment that your child's favourite television programme is about to start.

■ Choose books that are not too challenging – the interest level needs to be right (so your child is motivated) but with an easy-to-read vocabulary.

■ Choose books that match your child's interests (if they insist on dinosaurs or princesses every time, it doesn't matter; comics are perfectly fine too, so long as they do not consist of pictures without *any* text!)

■ Use the reading sessions to read for *pleasure* and to understand the *meaning* of the text. So, when your child comes to a word he or she cannot quickly sound out, simply read the word for your child. Avoid saying, 'Go on, try it out,' because that interrupts the flow of the sentence. You want to keep the flow going and to teach your child to read *fluently* rather than to think 'word by word'.

■ Make a note of any word that your child struggles with (in a notebook or on a file card); on another occasion you can go back to the word and teach it as a spelling (see page 178). This is a useful way of building up and consolidating reading vocabulary.

■ If your child is a somewhat reluctant reader, consider a structured reward (or incentive) scheme (see page 218).

Teenagers may need a little more encouragement to go back to doing some reading aloud with a parent. Explain that your aim is for fluency, for extending vocabulary and for practising comprehension (see page 173). A reward system (see page 219) may really be what you need in order to tip the balance in favour of co-operation.

Reinforce the reading your child is doing with teachers

Ask the teacher what your child is working on in reading and to give you some things to do at home. Perhaps use a special notebook to keep track from week to week.

For **younger children** you could:

- read simple books of one or two sentences per page that match the reading scheme
- reinforce the sight word vocabulary the teacher has been building up
- practise the letters and letter sounds that the teacher has been working on

You could also play some phonological (sound-based) games with your child. Here are some suggestions:

- Ask how many words your child can think of that begin with the 'ss' sound. (You need to know how to pronounce the sounds – remember the 'schwa', see page 26.)
- What words can your child think of that rhyme with 'day', 'mat', 'pen', and so on?
- Ask your child what is the beginning (and end and middle) sound in 'pen', and other words.
- Say the phonemes in a word very slowly and ask your child to 'blend' them together to make the word (s-t-i-ck makes 'stick').
- Ask your child to take away the beginning (or end) sounds of a word ('bat' without the 'b' sound says 'at', 'meet' without the 't' sound says 'me').

For **older children** it is still important to back up and work with what the literacy support teacher is doing. For example, this could involve drawing your child's attention to common sounds in words and how they are represented by written letters. You might say 'write down the "st" sound then write down a word starting (or ending) with "st".' Here are some other common letter combinations to work on:

- consonant blends 'st', 'str', 'pl', 'gr' (for these each letter sound is heard)
- diagraphs 'sh', 'th', 'wh', 'ch' (for these the consonants combine to make a single overall sound)
- vowel combinations 'ea', 'ei', 'au', 'oo'

Also practise some rules of reading/spelling. For example:

- The 'magic e'. When an 'e' is added to the end of a three-letter consonant-vowel-consonant word like 'mad', the vowel sound changes from a short to a long one. So 'mad' turns to 'made'.
- Talk about word 'families' (sometimes known as analogies) such as words ending in '-ight' (light, fright, fight, sight), '-tion' (mention, fraction, station).
- Practise the irregular sight words such as 'was' and 'there'/'their' (see pages 176 and 177 for the list of key word spellings as many of these are irregular too).

For **teenagers** – and even for younger children – it may be that nothing specific is suggested; just lots of reading. But do stay in touch with the teacher and keep asking if, at *this* particular moment, there is any useful backup work you can do at home.

Make reading relevant to everyday life

What you do at home shouldn't just be confined to learning sessions. Reading is part of every aspect of our lives. So encourage your child to read (as appropriate for age):

- road signs
- destinations on the front of buses
- labels on goods in shops
- washing instructions inside clothes
- restaurant and café menus
- television programme lists
- interesting websites on computers
- recipes
- food packet labels

Try to take a casual approach so that it is not too obvious that you are making your child read more – it shouldn't feel like work if you hope to make reading a regular part of your child's life. So, for example, get your child to cook a meal with you. Read the instructions on packets and in the recipes together – you helping with difficult words if needed. Or, get your child to pair up with a favourite relative or family friend to look up information for, say, a school project or a family holiday.

Develop reading fluency

Help your child to move beyond a 'wooden' reading style (reading word by word, stumbling or repeating words) by reading dialogue. Use plays or sections of speech in novels to develop *inflection* (getting the tone, emphasis, loudness/softness, accent and style to fit in with the characters and content of what is being read). You could read one part yourself or get your child to read several. Get various family members involved in this too, making it a fun and enjoyable shared reading experience. This will have another spin-off benefit of improving language and comprehension. Teenagers are perhaps more likely to prefer this to more basic reading-aloud exercises, which may just have to be left to the special needs teacher.

Develop reading for meaning (comprehension)

Reading is not just about recognising and decoding words. Most of all it is about understanding the meaning of what is being read. Research has shown that there are two basic skills needed for good *reading comprehension* – the ability to read the words accurately in the first place, and good spoken language (especially vocabulary knowledge). It is much harder for children to understand what they are reading if they cannot read many of the words – so reading together to improve accuracy is extremely important. It is also critical to promote good spoken language skills (see page 187).

Check your child's *listening comprehension* – read a passage aloud, asking your child to listen carefully and to remember what is being read. Then you can either ask your child to tell you as much as possible about the passage or you can ask some specific questions (such as, for a story, who appeared in it, where it was set, what happened, what was the main point; for nonfiction the questions need to centre around the facts in the passage). Start with short and simple passages or stories (and make sure that they are interesting or fun) and gradually work towards longer and more complicated passages. You can start with a group of three to four sentences for a struggling seven year old, and move to half or three quarters of a page of small print for a teenager or more able child. If your child finds it difficult to understand a passage when only *listening* is involved, then it would be good to practise this lots before moving on to *reading* comprehension.

Once comfortable with listening comprehension and your child is moving on to reading passages, get him/her to read aloud to you; that way you can quickly pick up on any words that he/she is struggling to read. Simply supply the correct word to keep the flow going and to make the reading less of an effort. Then, as before, ask detailed, specific questions and/or get your child to tell you back the content in his or her own words.

For **teenagers and older children** with reasonable reading skills, photocopy a passage and ask your child to highlight (with a coloured highlighter, or by circling with a red pen or underlining) the *key points*. Your child should then reread the highlighted sections, as this 'rehearsal' or practice helps to reinforce the main points of the story or passage. You can then follow up with the story-recall or question-and-answer exercises as above. This is really useful, not only for developing reading comprehension but also for comprehension exercises where the child has to read the questions and then write down the answers; *written comprehension* is necessary for many subjects at school, so it is good to prepare the groundwork.

For older children and teenagers again, a reading comprehension 'exercise' can be taken beyond just understanding and remembering the facts of a passage. The skill of *inference* can be developed by asking your child what might happen next, or how a character might be feeling or thinking (where this is not stated) or what the aim or theme (again, when not given) might actually be. You could also ask your child to give alternative endings, or ask what he or she thought the outcome would be if something other than the action given in the passage had happened instead (for example, if the man had *not* tripped over the dog, then what might have happened?) This kind of exercise develops thinking and reasoning skills.

WHAT YOU CAN DO: SPELLING

Help with school spelling lists

Most **younger children** will come home from school with a regular spelling list, usually at the beginning of the week for a test at the end. These might be given with an inbuilt letter pattern or a spelling rule, which can make the list easier to learn. Sometimes the list seems random (though it may have come out of some particular class work or word frequency list). Here are some general tips:

- Start on day one. Don't leave the learning until the end of the week.
- Do a little learning every day, using the techniques we suggest below.
- Each day set your child a few new words to learn. Also test the knowledge of (and practise again) words learned the

previous day. Leave the last day to revise all the words and to do a practice test.

■ Use a reward system or, for younger children, a chart on the wall which shows spellings that have already been correctly learned, to help with motivation.

■ Remember, the teacher may well check the spellings again at a later date – and children with learning problems are frequently able to learn a list for a Friday test but have forgotten the words completely by the following Wednesday. So do hang on to the list and keep on checking and practising the words at intervals until they are *over-learned* – and are so firmly in your child's long-term memory that they are less likely to be forgotten. For children with learning difficulties this will mean lots of practice.

Build up a key words spelling vocabulary

The 100 most common words in the English language apparently make up *half* of all the words we read and write! If your child can master these, any problems with writing will be much reduced. Unfortunately, many of these words have irregular spellings and so are harder to learn. To help you help your child, you can find these 100 words in the three boxes below – taken from Jim Doyle's book *Dyslexia: An Introductory Guide* (© John Wiley & Sons Limited, 2002) reproduced with permission.

The first box has only 12 words – but these make up *one quarter* of everything we read and write:

a	and	he
I	in	is
it	of	that
the	to	was

When the next 20 words are added on, *one third* of all the words regularly needed for reading and writing are covered:

all	as	at	be	but
are	for	had	have	him
his	not	on	one	said
so	they	we	with	you

And by the time you add the remaining words, the 100 words together make up 50 per cent of all the words we read and write:

about	an	back	been	before
big	by	call	came	can
come	could	did	do	down
first	from	get	go	has
her	here	if	into	just
like	little	look	made	make
me	more	much	must	my
no	new	now	off	only
or	our	other	out	over
right	see	she	some	their
them	then	there	this	two
when	up	want	well	went
were	what	where	which	who
will	your	old		

There should be no pressure for your child to learn these all at once. As for the spelling lists, build up slowly (start with the first list for those who need it), rehearse regularly, use a reward system – and encourage your child to practise using the words in sentences and stories.

'Over-learn' the spellings needed for each academic subject

When **older children** study subjects at school like geography, history or science, they need to spell accurately the (often technical) words that are specific to those subjects. For instance, they may find that in geography they have to write over and over again words like 'contour', 'temperature' or 'volcano', and in physics words such as 'electricity' and 'magnetism'. Together with your child, make a list of the most important words for each academic subject. Keep the list handy and carry on practising until these are over-learned (and the exams are in the past – and passed!)

Teach good spelling techniques

Learning a spelling list

Look out for *spelling patterns*, such as common word beginnings (un-, dis-, pre-) and endings (-tion, -ed, -ight), and draw your child's attention to these (and think together of some other words that might fit the pattern too). Ask your child to describe the pattern back to you – so he or she is *actively* understanding and learning.

Use a multisensory approach

Use the senses of seeing, hearing, saying and writing the word to be learned. So what your child needs to do is:

- *Look* at the (printed) word.
- *Say* the word out loud and hear it said (if your child can read the word, start with this – or say it for your child straight away if he or she can't read it).
- *Write* the word down.

Simultaneous oral spelling

The multisensory approach often incorporates another spelling technique known as *simultaneous oral spelling (SOS)*. For this your child needs to:

- *Remember* the word – and *cover* it with hand (or paper).
- *Write* the word from memory and *as each letter is being written say its letter name* (NB not the letter sound – so 'zed' not 'zz'). Usually a child says the letter name aloud but with practice this can be 'under the breath'.
- *Check* the word is written correctly (remove the covering hand).
- *Repeat* the whole process *at least three times*.

More repetitions with checks need to be made if your child makes an error in the spelling; keep going for as long as needed until the spelling is correct three tries in a row (do some easier words in between and keep going back to the spellings that are hard to learn). Practise the spelling at regular intervals over the following days, weeks and months to make sure the spelling is over-learned.

Learning difficult words

For long or difficult words here are some extra techniques that can be used to help to remember the spelling:

- Words within words – some words have other, shorter real words embedded in them that, hopefully, the child already knows how to spell (and, if not, teach these first). Some examples are:

  window　　　　**less-on**　　　mis**for-tune**
  co-ope**rate**　　　re**treat**ed

- Make up a funny sentence where each word begins with each of the letters of the word to be learned. This is especially useful for long and/or irregular words. Some examples are:
  'because': **b**ig **e**lephants **c**an **a**dd **u**p **s**o **e**asily
  'diarrhoea': **d**ashing **i**n **a** **r**eal **r**ush, **h**urry **o**r **e**lse **a**ccident

■ Use a rhyme or song with the spelling as part of it. For example (from 'The Jumblies'): 'They went to sea in a sieve, they did, in a s – ie – ve' (each letter name is spoken in the rhythm: 's', pause, 'i', 'e', pause, 'v', 'e'). The rule 'i before e except after c' is a common and useful rhyme too. Miss Honey in Roald Dahl's *Matilda* (Jonathan Cape Ltd and Penguin Books Ltd) sang out the letter names – for example to spell the word 'difficulty':

Mrs D, Mrs I, Mrs F-F-I
Mrs C, Mrs U, Mrs L-T-Y!

Use computers to help with spelling

Computer software games are not only fun but can also be used to teach or reinforce spelling and reading. A particularly good one is Wordshark (published by White Space and available from LDA, see page 231), which has sharks swimming across the screen gobbling up letters. The games are graded for different levels of difficulty. Touch Type Read and Spell is an excellent computer spelling programme too; children learn spelling patterns alongside typing skills. (See Organisations and Resources on page 227 for further programmes.)

For **older children** whose spelling errors are phonetically consistent – that is, the word when read *sounds* like the target word but is still incorrect (such as 'dream' spelled 'dreem' or 'dreme') – the spellchecker on the work processing package is likely to be helpful in coming up with the correct spelling. Unfortunately, the spellchecker does not *always* work, as the child may have to choose which word is correct from a number of options – and this may not be easy for some – but also because sometimes incorrect spellings are real words in themselves. At least it can be a help sometimes and it does draw attention to the fact that an error has been made. Your child can then consider what might be wrong and try again.

Get your child into the dictionary habit

Some dictionaries are specially designed for poor spellers. The dyslexia-friendly *ACE Dictionary* is perhaps the best known. For this to be helpful, however, a child has to have a certain minimum level of spelling ability – but anyone beyond the early stages should find this approach useful. So when your child asks you how to spell a word, suggest that you together look it up in the dictionary. You will need to practise doing this quite a bit before your child starts to reach for the dictionary without prompting, but it is a great idea to use such a special dictionary as a stepping stone to the conventional type. The *ACE Dictionary* works well because the vowels are coded *aurally* (according to their sounds) rather than *visually* (according to the spelling pattern). There is an easy-to-read index page showing how the first vowel in any word could sound. All the child needs to do is look down a column for the first letter of the word then across the line for the first vowel sound to find the right page for the spelling. The word can then be found easily in the short list on that page. There is even a small picture of an animal at the bottom of each page to help the child know what vowel sound to expect – for example, a picture of an eagle accompanied by the sentence, 'In these words you can hear the vowel sound ee as in eagle.'

Help your child build up a personal spelling dictionary

This can be done in an exercise book divided into the 26 letters of the alphabet. Some letters, such as 's' and 't', might need several pages, while letters that start few words, such as 'x', 'y' and 'z', can be put together on a single page. With the exercise book, the order of the letters is built in and may therefore help the more disorganised or younger child. Alternatively, file-cards can be used and kept in a box with a separate card for each word. The cards are best stored in alphabetical order with a coloured divider to separate the spellings starting with different letters. Whichever method is used, a definition (and even a picture for **younger children**) is helpful. With the card system it is easy to write the meaning of the word on the back, so the side with the spelling on it looks uncluttered. This system is also more flexible.

Cards can be taken out for extra practice in reading or spelling – or for checking that the child knows the meaning. Words can be collected for their interest value, and so vocabulary is extended (and **teenagers** are readier to 'buy into' an interesting word collection that they can even use to show off and test the family with, than a spelling list).

Encourage proofreading

When your child has produced a piece of writing, encourage a reread with an eye to picking up any spelling errors. You (and teachers) can help by making a mark in the margin against any line with a spelling error (noting the number of errors). Your child has to work out which word is wrong. If this approach is a little demoralising (especially if many errors are being flagged up), you can instead put ticks in the margin to show that there are no spelling errors in a line – and call it a 'good spellings line' rather than an 'error-free line'. As your child becomes more practised in picking up spelling errors by reading carefully through the work and checking key words especially, then the margin prompting can be dropped. It is important, though, that the 'checking habit' is continued long term. You could use a Post-It note, say, on your child's pencil case, saying something along the lines of 'Finished? Now check!' Other errors to be picked up by proofreading are those of punctuation and grammar.

Some means of motivating your child to carry out checks can be helpful. For **young children**, ticks can be added up for a small reward. **Teenagers and older children** might need a more sophisticated system. Rewards could be given for spending *time* checking rather than on success in being error free. To do this a kitchen timer could be set for, say, five minutes of checking time at the end of each piece of written work, with a reward of some kind given for doing this (prompted – or with a greater reward if this is done unprompted). (See page 219 for how to set up a reward system.) It might help in any case to discuss with your child how he or she would like this organised.

WHAT YOU CAN DO: WRITING

Getting the physical part right

Before even thinking about writing, look at how your child is sitting, the angle of the paper and the way he or she holds the pen/pencil (pencil grip). Bear in mind that children who are left-handed can find learning to write hard, and they are more likely to have an awkward pencil grip than right-handers. Some children get into the habit of sitting badly, slouching over their work or even writing in the 'wrong' place like the floor or bed. The best position to write well is at a table or desk, using a chair of the right height with a supporting back.

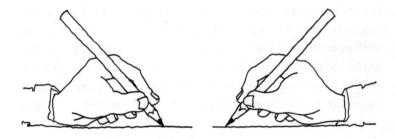

Correct pencil grip

Next, look at the position of the paper. This will vary according to whether the child is left- or right-handed, but the best position is a slight slant (a top left to bottom right diagonal for right-handers and a top right to bottom left for left-handers). This allows the arm to relax as the table will support it, and the hand and arm will be in a straight line with each other. It is possible to buy wedge-shaped boards to put the paper on; this raises the top of the paper and makes it even more comfortable for the child to write and to see easily what he or she is writing.

Paper placed in the correct position for left-handers

Holding the pen or pencil in a comfortable way is important. But really the only window of opportunity to make sure your child has the best grip is in the early school years – between the ages of four and seven. After that it can be very difficult, even impossible, to change an awkward pencil grip – and your child (and you) will just have to find ways round improving the writing, regardless of the grip. The main thing is that the child should feel relaxed and comfortable while writing. The best grip is called a tripod grip as the pencil is supported by three fingers. The pencil should be held on the coloured part, not too low down and onto the point. The pencil is held between the thumb and the index finger with the middle finger supporting from beneath. Rubberised pencil grips or pens and pencils with triangular shafts built in can encourage a good hold.

If your child is working with a physiotherapist or occupational therapist, it is very likely that they will want you to do some physical exercises with your child at home. They will also give you much helpful advice on the physical side of writing, including what pens and pencils would be especially useful for your child.

Getting the mechanics right

In the primary school, handwriting skills are taught and practised, but by secondary school it is likely that only those with severe difficulties will receive any assistance. The style of hand-writing can vary from school to school – but the class teacher or SENCO should be able to give you a printed sheet of letters to work from at home. **Younger children** who are moving from print to cursive writing may need help from the teacher, with you doing the back-up practice at home. Worksheets for tracing and copying letters are useful.

Tips for *older children*

- Neaten and speed up writing by having your child copy and continue letter patterns in a lined exercise book.
- Use paper with a printed margin to help presentation; suggest that your child puts his or her finger on it to help start each first letter of the line right next to the margin line.
- Either use a ballpoint pen with an ink eradicator or encourage your child to cross out words with errors neatly using a small line rather than writing over them.
- Practise copying passages (from a book or newspaper) as this does not involve thinking about anything other than the mechanics of the writing and presentation. The next stage is for your child to practise writing while you dictate a passage so that he or she gets to think about spelling and punctuation as well as the mechanics of writing.
- Do 'beat the clock' exercises to build up speed and fluency. Ask your child to copy (and later on dictate to him or her) five sentences as fast as he or she can. Record his or her time (a stopwatch or kitchen timer would be useful), make a note of the time in seconds and maybe keep it on a chart (for instance, Day 1, time =   ; Day 2, time =   , and so on). This gives your child both feedback and an incentive to see if he or she can beat the previous time. Try the same five sentences for, say, four consecutive days so that the number of words won't make a difference to the time taken to write them. Then start again with new sentences, so the exercise doesn't get boring.
- For the reluctant writer, build in an incentive programme

– for instance, giving rewards for *trying hard* with writing or for the amount of time you agree to work together on it (which may be no more than five minutes) – and give extra rewards for any signs of improvement in presentation/legibility.

What to do about persistent illegible handwriting

Some children never achieve legible handwriting even if they get a lot of help from home and school. Many of these children find it easier to print rather than use cursive writing – because it's easier for others, and even themselves, to read. This is perfectly reasonable. They can even become quite fast at printing, but they are most unlikely to write as fast as if they used cursive script. Older poor writers using a printing script should be given extra time in exams.

The alternative to handwriting is using the computer. This is especially useful for homework, coursework, projects, stories and essays. Handwriting will still be needed, for example in maths and science and for work using printed sheets. It is good to develop both writing and keyboard skills alongside each other. All children should be taught *touch typing* as it is such an essential skill. It allows them to keep their eye on what they are writing, to work more quickly and to think in sentences rather than word by word. The earlier children learn to touch type the better – it is very difficult to undo 'hunt and peck' typing techniques! Ask if school runs a touch-typing course, but bear in mind that one session per week at school will not in itself turn your child into a proficient touch typist. Alternatively, there may be afterschool courses such as Touch Type Read and Spell, based on the Alpha to Omega spelling scheme or software programmes such as Nessy Fingers (see page 230 for details). Back it up at home with regular practice, and encourage your child not to look down at his or her fingers while typing. Of course, some children, especially those who have marked dyspraxia, may not find learning to type as easy as other children. However, it is worth persisting because their handwritten efforts may be impossible to decipher.

Some children with serious handwriting difficulties and who are practised in using a computer for their work may be allowed to word process their answers in certain exams. Children need to have a good typing speed if this is to be worthwhile and for the accommodation to be granted. Some children with particularly severe handwriting problems will be able to use a laptop even for class work – though for note-taking they need to be very fast touch typists. Using a computer in the classroom and for exams is likely to be encouraged only for secondary school-age children, as younger children need to persist with handwriting for a little longer.

WHAT YOU CAN DO: LANGUAGE

Talk – and listen

Talk, talk, talk with your child. This is the best way of promoting his or her language. The more your child hears the spoken word, the better he or she will develop communication skills and increase knowledge. Include your family and friends, and your children's friends – together make language part of a fun social experience. Listening is important too – and it's a two-way process. Listening to your child will help you know what he or she understands and what help is needed. Your child's listening to you not only helps with understanding but also develops good concentration. And, of course, if your child feels that he or she is being heard, it will be good for family relationships too.

*Tips for helping **younger children** improve their vocabulary, grammar and comprehension*
Expand and recast what your child says. When your child says something with missing words or poor vocabulary, repeat it back in a slightly longer and more interesting way, taking the opportunity to correct any errors or to add interesting vocabulary. Obviously, you can't do this with everything your child says or be heavy handed about it. For instance, your child might say, 'I done my homework. I want a doughnut.' You could say,

'Fantastic. You have done your homework, so you can have a doughnut now. You can choose either a jam or a plain one.' And you can add in a joking way all kinds of mock-serious comments such as, 'Or maybe you would like to choose a delicious stripy monster cake or my wonderful feather-light rock cake?' What you are doing here is correcting a grammatical error ('I done' to 'I have done') and at the same time adding some interesting vocabulary. Judge carefully your child's level of understanding so he or she feels neither talked down to nor that the language is over his or her head.

Reflect and reinforce what your child says. This is a technique for children whose language problems mean that they rarely say more than single words or short phrases. When your child says a short but appropriate or sensible sentence, you simply repeat it back – this is the reflection part – and it helps to reinforce (or show) the child that he or she is speaking well. You then continue the conversation based on what your child has said, so helping to develop a flowing conversation. For instance, your child might say, 'We watched a video,' to which you reply, 'Oh, you watched a video at school today, did you? What was it about?'

Build up vocabulary using day-to-day conversation. Keep on pointing out:

- unfamiliar or unusual objects; name them and talk about them
- descriptive words covering tastes, textures, sounds, shapes and so on; for example, for sounds: screeching, soothing, whistling
- prepositions and relationship words such as 'next to', 'under', 'on top of', 'in between', 'beside'
- the vocabulary of feelings or emotions such as 'miserable', 'worried', 'elated', 'distraught'

Play games with words like taking turns to think up as many words as possible within a given category such as animals, colours, feelings, building materials, sports, clothing. Your child will probably name the simpler words but you can come up with more unusual examples to expand his or her vocabulary (for instance, for the category colour, your child might say 'yellow' and you can say 'indigo' or 'turquoise'). Another game is to show your child an interesting picture – say, cut from a magazine or in a book – and ask him or her to describe or tell you a story about the picture. Finally, try drawing a series of pictures that tell a story or cut them out of a comic book, put them out in a jumbled order, then get your child to put them in the right order and tell you the story in words.

If your child is seeing a speech and language therapist, ask for some further ideas and games for helping develop language at home.

Tips for older children and teenagers

- Pick a topic from the television or newspaper and talk about it with your child. This is good for stretching thinking skills, introducing new vocabulary and helping him or her to develop reasoned arguments.
- Plan to do some activity together with your child as often as you can – cooking is always good but outings to the library or a museum are a great opportunity for expanding vocabulary and broadening general knowledge.
- Play games like 'What am I talking about?' where you describe a particular activity or object without naming it and ask your child to tell you what it is. Also, 'I Spy' and charades are good games for helping children focus on object names. Another game is where a group of three or four people build up a story by each taking it in turn to come up with a sentence or idea. (For example, person one says: 'My mother went to the shops to buy …' Person two says: '… herself a belt. But on the way to the shopping centre something very strange happened.' Person three carries on with the story.)

Learn language through books

For younger children:

■ Read stories to your child – talk about them and ask questions about what you've read, and sometimes get your child to tell the story back to you.

■ Play story tapes – children love to have these repeated and they will pick up more things each time they listen. 'Listening Books' offers a library service of books or tapes/CDs for children with special needs (see page 229).

■ Make scrapbooks describing activities your child has been involved in, his or her interests and family events – concentrating particularly on vocabulary and colourful descriptions.

For older children and teenagers:

■ Encourage your child to read every day – if he or she is having difficulties with reading (and, of course, quite a lot of children with language difficulties do), get your child to listen to books on tapes – libraries and Listening Books have good selections of these.

■ Suggest your child writes a diary.

■ Play games like Scrabble where your child can learn more about vocabulary.

Note that all the suggestions about books that are in the Reading section, above, will also help with language. The section 'Develop reading for meaning (comprehension)' is especially relevant (see page 173). Also, get your child to build up a word bank for collecting words and expanding vocabulary – as described in the section 'Help your child build up a personal spelling dictionary' (see page 181).

WHAT YOU CAN DO: MATHS

Maths is the hardest subject for most parents to help their children with at home. You need to know your child's level, what is currently being taught at school and what methods are being used. And maths is a subject that is daunting for many parents who may themselves have been turned off it at school!

Work on maths specifics

For any specific areas of maths, talk to your child's teacher and get worksheets to practise at home. Look together at what areas and aspects your child is having difficulty with – and consider what strategies you can use to help at home. Here are some examples.

Counting skills

Make sure your child has built up good counting skills (some of this may apply only to a young child or those with very severe difficulties). Begin with counting in ones, forwards then backwards, up to 100. Then move to counting in twos, fives and tens before tackling other numbers like three and seven (these are all useful for multiplication). Coins will help with counting practice – with the added spin-off of linking maths with the real world of money.

Number bonds

Make sure number bonds are secure (number bonds are pairs of numbers that add up to a given number; number bonds to 10 means 8 + 2, 7 + 3, 5 + 5 and so on). Children need to be able to do this quickly without using their fingers. The number bonds develop out of counting and from simple addition. Knowing the basic number bonds is really important for speed of working later, as well as being the basis for complex maths. So you could regularly ask your child questions like, '8 plus what makes 10?' If your child is struggling with this, go back to learning the number bonds to 5. Once the bonds to 5 and to 10 are secure, you can move on in small steps to higher numbers. For **older children**, you could work on number bonds up to 50, or even 100.

Multiplication

For multiplication problems, draw up a tables grid to help understand the principles and to see the patterns. Then *lots* of practice

– it does help to rote learn tables, but this can be made more fun and more effective by chanting or singing. The grid below shows all the tables up to 10. When a number from the top row is multiplied by a number from the left-hand column, the answer can be found where they meet on the grid (so 5 x 2 = 10).

Tables Grid

	0	1	2	3	4	5	6	7	8	9	10
0	0	0	0	0	0	0	0	0	0	0	0
1	0	1	2	3	4	5	6	7	8	9	10
2	0	2	4	6	8	10	12	14	16	18	20
3	0	3	6	9	12	15	18	21	24	27	30
4	0	4	8	12	16	20	24	28	32	36	40
5	0	5	10	15	20	25	30	35	40	45	50
6	0	6	12	18	24	30	36	42	48	54	60
7	0	7	14	21	28	35	42	49	56	63	70
8	0	8	16	24	32	40	48	56	64	72	80
9	0	9	18	27	36	45	54	63	72	81	90
10	0	10	20	30	40	50	60	70	80	90	100

Memorising number facts

A technique for memorising number facts originated by Dr Colin Lane is 'self-voice echo™'. Most of us learn better from hearing information spoken in our own voices than when someone else is talking. So, to apply this to learning tables, the child should practise reciting the table 'under his or her breath'. It is helpful too for the child to tape him/herself reciting the tables and play them back while looking at the numbers on the page. This gives a *multisensory* learning experience.

Fractions

For fractions, cut up paper – and cakes, pieces of fruit, and so on – to illustrate the principles. Try to make your pieces look to scale – so a half is the size of a proper half of the whole. For example, cut a piece of paper into four equal pieces, each labelled ¼. Put two of these quarters together to show how they become a half. And now relate the physical pieces to how the fraction is written. Thus:

$$\frac{1}{4} \quad \text{add} \quad \frac{1}{4} \quad \text{makes} \quad \frac{2}{4} \quad \text{or} \quad \frac{1}{2}$$

one quarter add one quarter makes two quarters or one half

You can take the fractions a step further to do more complex adding and also subtracting.

Maths needs practice, practice, practice

Over the short and longer term, regular practice – and lots of it – is needed. Children with dyscalculia forget so quickly – even the maths they seem to have got the hang of. It is very demoralising for them, so it is much better to prevent the forgetting and the need to relearn by keeping the knowledge 'hot' through lots of practice.

Some tips for practising maths

- Practise daily any new concept or skill – for a period of, say, two weeks to begin with. Get the skill thoroughly learned – and even over-learned.
- Keep sessions short – 5–10 minutes is enough.
- Use homework materials, suggested worksheets from school, and commercially available worksheet-based books.
- Keep revising work – say every month or so – to make absolutely sure your child still remembers what to do. Practise the same techniques and types of sums over and over – don't *just* learn new ones and assume that something learned once will stick.
- You could try the worksheet-based commercial maths programme, called Kumon, which has centres throughout the country (see page 229 for contact details). Kumon maths is a systematic, graded and structured programme suitable for a wide ability and age range. It starts at a basic level for children with minimal mathematical skills and goes right through to GCSE and

A-level maths. It covers skills ranging from counting and number bonds to more complex operations such as short and long multiplication and division, fractions, decimals and algebra. Kumon involves a high degree of repetition and moves up in small steps so is great at making skills automatic. This also prevents the forgetting so typical of children with dyscalculia. Unfortunately, carrying on with the scheme might be a bit tedious for some children. Kumon's own incentive plan should help but you may want to add a home-based motivation scheme where you give rewards for the work done each day (see Chapter 11). Also, have breaks from Kumon from time to time. To make it more fun, organise for your child to do the daily exercises with friends – maybe while you prepare them a drink or a snack treat.

Maths is for everyday life

Maths is an essential part of all our lives and does not just exist in the abstract. So use every opportunity to practise the skills in real situations:

- Count out the change given back when shopping (for the younger ones) or calculate what change is owing (for the older and more able children).
- Calculate, when out shopping for clothes in the sales, how much money will be saved when the items are reduced by a certain percentage or amount.
- In the supermarket when buying in bulk, tell your child the price of a single item and ask what four, five or ten items, and so on, might cost (some of the harder ones might need pencil and paper).
- Practise using a calculator while out shopping. Get your child to add up the individual prices as you collect the goods – and see if his or her total matches what the till comes up with.
- Practise taking measurements. Use a tape measure to measure height, width and depth of just about anything –

and anyone. Make measurement comparisons – using words like longer/shorter, deeper/shallower, wider/narrower, bigger/smaller. Practise taking measurements when cooking. Get your child to weigh the ingredients in a recipe. Measure the liquids in a jug, cup or spoon. Again, use comparisons, with language such as more/less, heavier/lighter, fuller/emptier, and so on. Look at the cooking times needed for a particular dish and use a kitchen timer – this is good for practising and understanding time measurements too.

■ Practise understanding concepts of time. Encourage your child to mark his or her various activities on a calendar. Include longer-term things like the beginning and end of terms and family birthdays as well as planned activities such as outings, football practice, seeing friends, sleepovers and so on. Use the opportunity to teach, if still needed, the days of the week and the months and how they relate to a whole year. Calendars don't just teach children about time, but help them with organisational skills such as planning and thinking ahead too.

■ Encourage time management for travelling around. Look at bus and train timetables with your child. Plan journeys – talk about different ways of getting to their destination. Ask which route would take the shortest time (and, perhaps, which would be the cheapest too).

■ ■ ■

Children with learning difficulties find it hard to learn new things and to remember them. Parents aren't teachers – your job is to back up the work that's done in the classroom and with specialist teachers. The most important thing you can do is reinforce and practise skills – whenever you can but in a calm and relaxed way. Regular practice really is the key to remembering and moving forward. The hard work you put in now can produce spectacular results in the long term.

11

Working on Attention, Organisation and Study Skills

For a child with a specific learning difficulty, improving the relevant educational skills described in the last chapter is vitally important – but not the whole story. Your child's success in overcoming or compensating for his or her difficulties – and your success in helping – depend too on building up more general skills such as concentration/attention, study skills, motivation, organisation and planning, time management, revision and exam techniques. These skills can also make a huge difference to your relationship with your child – and to the sanity of the whole family. If these structures and skills are in place, learning becomes more routine and less of a source of strife. This will reduce your child's anxieties and potential unhappiness and encourage a positive feeling of being able to cope.

BUILD UP CONCENTRATION

Helping your child improve concentration benefits all academic subjects. It may be hard sometimes to know what comes first – a concentration difficulty or a learning difficulty. Children who are struggling with their work because they have a learning difficulty can readily become turned off, and lose focus and concentration. Other children, whose main problem is one of attention, miss out on what is being taught in class and so fall behind with their work. Either way, whether the concentration difficulty is the *cause* or *effect*, the things you can do to improve your child's ability to focus are much the same.

Some children will be able to improve attention and concentration by means of the ideas for motivation discussed on page 217. Other children whose concentration difficulties really get in the way of learning will need a *systematic concentration plan*. Set up a plan to extend concentration gradually – with tasks such as homework, number worksheet practice and reading/writing activities.

Tips for helping younger children improve their concentration

- Choose a quiet place to work where there are as few things to distract your child's attention as possible. Certainly no television or tempting toys and games!

- Think about what your child's concentration span is now – that is, the amount of time he or she can manage to stay on task, working on a formal activity. This may be as little as five minutes for a six year old with an attention problem, or 10 minutes for an eight year old. This is your 'baseline' – write it down.

- To lengthen your child's span, build up from the baseline in small, manageable steps to a longer period. So, from five minutes to six or seven, or from 10 to 12 minutes. Don't move on to a longer working time until your child can manage the shorter one comfortably and easily.

- Use a kitchen timer to mark the working period (the time your child is going to spend working). Avoid clocks and watches that might tempt your child to look at how much time has gone by, as this breaks concentration. Tell your child to work *as hard as he or she can* until the timer buzzer sounds – and that, if he or she does this, the time will seem to fly by very quickly. Do stick to the agreed time and don't be tempted to overstep it if your child is working well. Your child can always agree to reset the buzzer and do another session if he or she really wants.

■ If your child is very young or has a poor concentration span, stay close by while he or she works, as you may just need to remind him or her to keep on task. If your child's attention does start to wander, prompt by silently pointing your finger to the page he or she is working on. At the end of the session praise your child not only for successfully completing the work, but also for being so great at getting his or her attention back to the task in hand. As children get older, they should be able to be left on their own to do their work. This is what you should aim towards, though many children with ADHD will need close supervision and continued (gentle) prompting both at school and at home.

■ Leave your child working alone for only very short periods before you come back to check on how he or she is doing. Start with a couple of minutes and increase this if your child is managing well.

■ For the child with a poor working memory (see page 82), be extra sure to keep instructions short, repeat them if necessary (and get the child to repeat them too!) and use lots of memory joggers like counting blocks, multiplication table grids, calculators for maths and clips or stickers for place keeping.

■ Give your child a reward – and lots of praise – at the end of each session. For a child choosing to do an extra session, give a reward that is more than double that for one session, for further encouragement. If each session ends on a positive and happy note (with you pleased instead of cross and nagging your child to get on with it), then he or she will be much more likely to want to sit down and concentrate again.

Concentration tips for older children and teenagers

For older children and teenagers you do much the same thing, but expect them to continue working for longer and with a greater degree of independence. The things you can do to help are:

■ Discuss a plan with your child and agree the times. It is often best to suggest periods of, say, 15 minutes with rest breaks between each 15-minute period (of no more than a couple of minutes if your child is in the middle of an essay) and then a longer break after three-quarters of an hour or so. In the breaks some children will like to stretch their legs or even have some fresh air and a small snack. Encourage your child to be responsible for setting and resetting the kitchen timer, and to concentrate as hard as possible each time, so the actual time spent working *seems* shorter. Having your child involved in taking responsibility for work and time management is an important part of the motivation to work and the improvement of concentration.

■ Limit distractions. Your child needs to come to an understanding that being able to concentrate is much harder if there are external distractions. Mobile phone texting, iPod shuffling, watching television and doing computer games are best kept for your child to *reward him/herself* for completing the work.

COPE WITH HOMEWORK

Getting homework done can present challenges for any child, but is particularly a source of stress and difficulty for children with learning difficulties. It often brings them into conflict with parents and sometimes with school.

Children receive homework from about Year 1, when it may be little more than bringing a reading book home. Homework tasks increase throughout the secondary school years, and there may well be coursework assignments and projects to be completed, as well as shorter pieces of work.

The responsibility for homework at the secondary school age is the pupil's. If your child has not managed to get the work done within a reasonable period of time, then the teachers are the people whose job it is to step in and decide what to do. It may be that, for children with a learning difficulty, the amount or content of the homework is overwhelming; a sensible solution would be to set a child who is struggling an amount or level of work that is within his or her capability – but this has to be discussed and agreed with the teacher or teachers concerned. If, on the other hand, a child 'can't be bothered' or defiantly refuses to work, then there will be sanctions – which *school* rather than you will apply. If you get to this stage, however, there are clearly behavioural and emotional issues that need addressing, and a consultation with a recommended professional (a designated teacher or counsellor) might be helpful. Look at the section on motivation to see how to get round children who are resistant to doing homework (see page 217). To avoid difficulties in the first place, or indeed to resolve a more recent crisis, it is important to help children develop good 'homework habits' and be organised with their work.

Create the homework habit

Homework needs to become routine and be seen as an extension of the school day. Below are some tips to help develop (or redevelop) good habits. To make the suggestions work you will need, for **younger children**, to give clear instructions and explanations about how the homework arrangements are to be set up. **Older children** should be much more involved in the organisation of homework; they need to see this as something helpful for them, a way of getting around their learning difficulties and developing their own personal skills, and not something imposed on them for the sake of it. Planning together with your child and making an agreement or 'contract' for which both you and your child put in some effort – your child organises and does the work and you, the parent, offer support, praise and rewards – is a useful approach with older children. Make sure you set this up in a way that sounds positive and appealing. So for your child to acquire good homework habits he or she will need to:

■ *Agree with you on a good place to work.* Somewhere quiet if possible, free of tempting distractions, at a desk or table with good lighting. Some children and parents find the kitchen table ideal, despite a general hubbub, as parents can more easily help out with problems and refocus attention as necessary. Other children work better alone (but you may need to take further action if your child insists on being shut up in his or her room and fails to get on with work – a structured motivation scheme might be used to get around this problem without causing too much strife).

■ *Begin homework within 15–20 minutes of return from school.* Return home times can vary hugely and depend on distance to travel, involvement in after-school clubs and activities, and so on, so it does not make sense to start at a fixed time. It is also best to avoid relaxing activities like the television and computer until after the homework has been done.

■ *Stay in the clothes worn to school* to reinforce the idea that homework is part of the school day.

■ *Start each evening of homework by making a plan of what has to be done.* Your child needs to sort out what subjects need doing, how much time is required and that the necessary books and equipment are to hand before starting work. A filled-in homework diary may be very useful for younger children, and is essential for older children. If an important book or detail of the homework has been forgotten, encourage your child to call up a school mate for the details – and do reward your child for doing this rather than getting cross with him or her for forgetting in the first place.

■ *Decide how the time should be organised.* **Young children** will probably manage all their homework in a single short session – the problem for younger ones is often getting down to work in the first place rather than actually doing it, or trying to do it. **Older children and teenagers** will require breaks to keep going – mini-breaks can be taken, say after each 15 minutes, with a longer break after a section or whole piece of work has been completed.

■ *Remind him/herself to take each bit a step at a time* so the whole does not seem overwhelming; if something is too hard, your child should not be anxious but try to work steadily and do as much as is reasonably possible.

■ *Be rewarded* for trying hard, being co-operative, completing work, being organised with the books and materials – and, for **older children**, also for meeting deadlines, remembering to give completed homework in on time, bringing back and filling in the homework diary. (See page 219 for how to set up a reward scheme.)

If it proves really hard for you and/or your child to set up and successfully manage the homework, it may be that there is a school-based homework club that your child can attend. This might save much worry on your part as well as avoiding the nagging and conflict that may follow a child's refusal to do homework.

Set up a homework organisation chart
Overleaf is a blank homework chart for you to copy. The explanation follows.

Homework Organisation Chart

DAY GIVEN (Circle day)   **Monday Tuesday Wednesday**

SUBJECT 1.........................

Date given	Work given	Work due in by	Work done by	Work done in advance	Handed in on time	Mark/ Comment

SUBJECT 2.........................

Date given	Work given	Work due in by	Work done by	Work done in advance	Handed in on time	Mark/ Comment

Thursday Friday

SUBJECT 3...........................

Date given	Work given	Work due in by	Work done by	Work done in advance	Handed in on time	Mark/ Comment

SUBJECT 4...........................

Date given	Work given	Work due in by	Work done by	Work done in advance	Handed in on time	Mark/ Comment

The charts are set up for your child to keep a daily record of homework information so that both he or she and you can see at a glance how your child is managing throughout the term. It works on the principle that older children and teenagers can be given up to four separate pieces of homework on any one day (marked 'Subject 1...' to 'Subject 4...' on the chart); children know which subjects are likely to attract homework on each day as this is linked to the school timetable. The chart needs to be copied *five* times – so do use a large piece of paper (A4 or bigger). The actual day of the week can be circled on the top of each page (for example, for Monday's homework page put a circle around 'Monday'), and details of the homework regularly given on that day written into the SUBJECT space at the top of each subject box (obtained by dividing the paper into four equal parts). Each subject box needs to be divided into columns, as follows:

1. DATE GIVEN

This is the date on which the particular homework is handed out. There should be a date written in for every day of the term (as you are keeping a record of all the homeworks of the term).

2. WORK GIVEN

There should be enough information for your child to be clear what the homework was, even three weeks or more later. So if the homework is an essay, your child should write 'essay on...'. Learning-only (as opposed to written) homework should be noted as well. If no homework is set, 'NONE SET' should be written into this column. The aim here is for your child to help him/herself make sure that homework set cannot be forgotten!

3. WORK DUE IN BY

Put in the date that the homework is due in to help keep track of how much time there is to do the work. This needs to link in with the next two columns (4 and 5).

4. WORK DONE BY

Put in the date when the work was completed to show whether it was done within the expected time.

5. WORK DONE IN ADVANCE

Put in the number of days between the work being completed and the date it is due to be handed in. This is particularly relevant to longer-term projects but also to work expected to be handed in at school around a week later. The child who gets on quickly with newly set work, without leaving it all for the last moment, should be rewarded (see page 218). The amount of reward should increase with the speed and enthusiasm of getting down to the work. For work due in the next day or day after, the concept of 'done in advance' probably won't apply – especially if you have been making sure homework gets completed. But the next column may well be important to get the disorganised student thinking more for him/herself about the homework process.

6. HANDED IN ON TIME

Put a tick if done. This is to encourage children who have done their homework not to fail to give it in on time.

7. MARK/COMMENT

Keeping track of what the teachers think of the work on a day-to-day and subject basis means that you will not need to wait for an end-of-term report or other contact from the school to know how everything is progressing. This is really important, not just for you but also for your child to know. Keeping track of marks/grades will enable your child to know at a glance whether he or she is doing well enough – or needs to ask for some help. It also means that your child can see if a teacher who seems suddenly cross or gives a low mark in a half-term or end-of-term report has been fair or not. Your child can see which subjects might be most affected by his or her specific learning difficulty, and by how much.

On a practical note, the mark will have to be added in to the chart on the day your child gets the work back from the teacher. If no comment or mark is given, this should be recorded too. You want to encourage your child to be honest and not 'lose' returned work that has received a low mark. If you link this chart with a reward scheme (essential, really, for it to be effective in improving organisation) you can reward your child for honesty for writing in a poor mark. You can also reward him or her for taking some action to make things better – say, by talking to the teacher, by letting you help him or her to understand how to go about it, by going through the work together, or by getting help from another source. If your child becomes upset by including negative comments or low marks, leave these out – it is better to emphasise the positive and reward for achievements.

Here is an example of a partially completed chart, for one subject only:

DAY GIVEN (Circle day) (**Monday**) **Tuesday Wednesday**

SUBJECT 1 - ENGLISH

Date given	Work given	Work due in by	Work done by	Work done in advance	Handed in on time	Mark/ Comment
07/05	Comprehension exercise, page 12	08/05	08/05	—	√	8/10 good
14/05	Read set short story; precis	21/05	19/05	√ 2 days in advance	√	5/10 aim to develop more detail
21/05	Learning spelling list for test	28/05	28/05	—	√	17/20

REVISE AND PASS EXAMS

These suggestions are really only for **older children and teenagers** (11 years and upwards), who are expected to do formal tests and exams.

There are two stages to passing exams – how to manage the revision period beforehand and then what to do in the exams themselves.

Revision

First, help your child to *know what the syllabus is*. This means checking that everything has been covered (in class or out) that he or she is going to be examined on. Get your child to check through his or her files to see what the topics are, and make sure he or she catches up on any work missed for one reason or another. Your child should also check with the teacher what topics are going to be covered in the exam, and perhaps ask for a typed list of these (helpful for both child and parents).

Then s*et up a revision chart* (see below) and link it in with a motivation scheme.

Making and using a revision chart

The revision chart is a way of keeping a record of work that needs doing, and work done from the start of the revision period right up to the time of the exams themselves. It is not based on a timetable of work to get done in any one day – all too often such timetables don't work, despite good intentions, and they may even lead to demoralisation because of failure to stick to the plan. The plan proposed here aims to get around these problems. It involves making a chart to:

- record the syllabus or topics covered by the exam
- keep a record of each time any work is done on a particular topic (in order to make sure nothing is missed; to remind your child of what might need going over again; and to increase motivation by providing visual proof of success/work done)

■ provide an easy means of linking work done with reinforcing rewards for the efforts made

On a large sheet of paper draw lines to make a column for the individual topics going down the page, and for dates going across the page. This will form squares that can be coloured in each time a topic is worked on, and will show the day on which it is done. Each school subject will need a separate chart, so make sure there is enough space at the top of each page to note the subject to which that chart refers. It is often best if you, the parent, set these charts up so your child does not spend ages getting the chart up and running at the expense of doing the work (though many youngsters are such whizzes on the computer they will be able to get everything done faster and better than you).

Write in (together with your child) the topic list in reasonably fine detail, preferably grouped under headings. Then write in all the dates until the exam. Suggest that revision is done in 15-minute chunks of good concentration. When your child has done 15 minutes of work, he or she can take a short break and start afresh. Then, if your child can 'steal' another 15 minutes of time before supper – or on the bus, or before starting some activity – it will be even better. In this way, time spent working can mount up without it feeling such a great effort. Kitchen timers help prevent time being wasted on clock watching and give the child control.

If your child feels that he or she wants to do more than 15 minutes in one day on an individual topic, it can be written into a single square following the key. So if your child is, say, writing an essay on a topic and spends 30 minutes on it, use the colour (black in our chart) to show he or she has spent longer. This makes it clear that your child has earned two units of reward – each 15 minutes of work done should be linked to one unit of reward.

Here is an example:

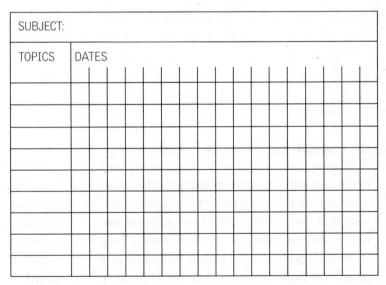

SUBJECT: Geography																	
TOPICS	DATES																
	8/4	9/4	10/4	11/4	12/4	13/4	14/4	15/4	16/4	17/4	18/4	19/4	20/4	21/4	22/4	23/4	24/4
Volcanoes																	
Rivers	�																
Coasts		▪															
Industry		▪															
Aid	▪		▪	■													
Map work																	

You can copy the following blank revision chart.

SUBJECT:																	
TOPICS	DATES																

KEY: Colour in the square for the date on which you revise a particular topic. Work in intervals of 15 minutes, but when you spend more than this amount of time on one topic, indicate this by colouring in the appropriate square with a different colour.

▪ = 15 minutes   ■ = 30 minutes

More revision tips to pass on to your child

■ *Make written notes* in the run-up to an exam and talk it through too (with you, with friends, to him/herself) so the learning is multisensory (look, hear, write) – making remembering easier. Closer to the date of the exam the notes can be reduced and summarised by writing them down in the form of short bullet points on file cards. The preparation of the cards should further help your child to get the information firmly fixed in his or her memory.

■ *Make big wall posters* using bright colours and clear but fun lettering to flag up hard-to-remember information or to display large amounts of information that it is helpful to see all together on one page (for example, French verbs). Also, use smaller Post-Its to stick on the wall (in the bedroom, on the bathroom mirror or on the fridge) for short items like geography or science facts. These wall notes can be seen as the 'no work' part of revision (always good for the reluctant student). Explain to your child that all he or she has to do is look at the notes and posters and read them through – while cleaning teeth, brushing hair, listening to music or just standing. Merely looking at the facts will act as a memory jog – and firm up the memory traces in his or her brain.

■ *Play 'revision games'* to improve memory. Actively trying to remember the facts before checking to see the information has been correctly learned is even better than just reading through. Encourage your child to try to recall from memory the information on a Post-It or on a page – and to reward him/herself with an imaginary pat on the back for success. (You could also play this game with your child and make sure the rewards are worthwhile.)

■ *Make up rhymes for hard-to-learn facts* and use mnemonics for remembering lists.

■ *Use a dictating/recording machine* if your child finds note-writing hard, and get him or her to play it back when lying in bed (or wherever).

■ *Relax and de-stress about exams.* In the days and weeks before the exam, set aside time for relaxation. Some children might find it helpful to listen to a special relaxation tape or to soothing music while trying to relax muscles. On the night before the exam, encourage your child to have an early night (following a final quick read-through of the bullet points on his or her revision file cards). Also, suggest that your child avoids eating too much just before an exam – to increase alertness. A small portion of slow-release carbohydrate food (such as a bowl of muesli-type cereal or a sandwich with wholemeal bread) is a good option, while avoiding sugar and fizzy drinks.

Get the most out of exams

For the exam itself, remind your child beforehand to:

- Read each question carefully at least twice.
- Underline the key points in the question (wherever this is possible). If there is more than one issue to be taken into account in a single question, number them (numbers written in circles are the clearest – for example, ①).
- Make sure that the length and detail of the answer match the number of marks allocated to the question.
- Make a plan for essays or longer answers – this should take no more than a couple of minutes. For those who are good at thinking in logical, ordered sequences, a list of key words or phrases can work well. For those who find it difficult to decide on what order things should go in, a **'key words spider'** works better (see overleaf).
- Check the answers – make sure all questions have been answered and use the opportunity to add in any points that were missed the first time around. Then do a quick check to make sure that spelling (especially important words) and punctuation are correct. Many children with specific learning difficulties will have been granted extra time to do these things as well as for compensating them for their slow speeds of processing and writing.
- Enjoy the challenge of the exam! Remind your child that doing the best he or she can is fine. The real work was the revision beforehand. And plan a fun treat for afterwards.

How to make a key words spider

1. The essay or story title should be thought of as the body of the spider. Important words in the title should be underlined. (In an exam the title may not need to be written out again to make the plan.)

2. The main ideas should be jotted down around the spider's body to make the first section of each leg, as they come to mind. The focus here is to get the ideas down quickly. Ordering into a sequence comes later. Key word or phrases are used here and will form the main paragraphs.

3. The legs each have a second section. At the end of these are added key words or phrases that will be useful to include in each main paragraph. This is the moment to think about spelling important words.

4. Putting the information from each leg into the best order is the next stage. It is easiest to number these by putting each number in a circle.

5. As the answer is being written, the plan should be looked at often and any forgotten bits added in as they come to mind. After this the writing of the essay should be straightforward, as there will be no need to think about its structure, only how to express the ideas.

6. An introduction and a conclusion will generally be needed also to complete the essay.

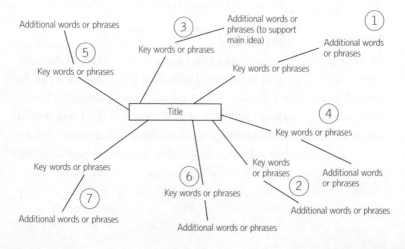

BEAT DISORGANISATION – DEVELOP SELF-ORGANISATION

Self-organisation is a vital skill to acquire during the school years – it is needed not just for school but for later post-school courses, jobs and careers too. You do not want to be endlessly behind your child, urging him or her to get on with homework and making time you do not have to do things for him or her. Getting the homework habit is a good start, but becoming fully and independently organised requires lots of other skills and habits, and it is worth starting to develop these skills as early as you can. Here are some tips to help your child become organised.

Encourage regular routines

Routines are important for bedtimes, meal times and, of course, homework and study sessions. The inbuilt predictability takes away stress and makes it easier to keep on top of things. With **younger children** it is relatively easy to establish the routines, especially if a reward system is used to get them into place. **Older children** may be more resistant (especially if they feel badly about themselves because they have a specific learning difficulty) and you can't force them. Instead use explanations and discussions to help your child see how routines will benefit not just him or her but all the family as well, and use rewards to motivate your child (and the rest of the family) to stick to them.

Teach timetabling skills

Most important is the timetable of the school day. Make sure your child has a small version of the school timetable that can be carried around in a pocket. Children who have marked difficulties with organisation (and who may have dyspraxia) will find it easier to scan the timetable if each subject has its own colour (such as red for history, blue for maths …). Some find it useful also to make their own timetables or charts for planning homework, holiday work, coursework and revision. These need to be easily visible and near where your child works at home to be of maximum value.

Teach short- and long-term time-management skills

The suggestions for organising time in the section on homework are also part of time management. Managing an evening's
homework is *short-term* time management. *Longer-term* time
management is important too; to make sure that coursework
and projects are finished and handed in on time, further
action is required, such as the homework organisation chart (see
pages 204–5).

Set up a subject filing system

So many children with learning difficulties end up with their
school work and class notes crumpled up at the bottom of a bag
(because they have lost their exercise books or files) and/or
strewn around school and home all jumbled up. These bits of
paper will end up lost and be hard to make head or tail of when
someone (you, probably) tries to sort them out.

Involve your child in finding an appealing filing system – like
sets of coloured box files, or coloured envelope files, with each
colour matching the chosen colour for the subject on the
timetable, or a portable concertina file or even a single file with
dividers. Together, set up the system (ask an obliging teacher to
help if your child refuses your assistance), file his or her work and
label each section clearly. Make sure everything is easy for your
child to find. If using a ring binder file, use stick-out coloured
tabs on the sides of the dividers for even easier access and visibil-
ity of sections. When considering what sort of file to use, it is
worth noting that straight-sided rings cause less of a problem
with paper getting torn around the ring holes, so needing
gummed reinforcers, than curved rings. However, straight-sided
rings are usually only found on larger files that are therefore
harder to carry around.

Children who are disorganised tend to lose their school bags
and their work, so it is best to set up a system with larger files or
boxes for keeping the year's work together at home, with only
small files to transport stuff needed for school that day or week.
Your child will also need an easily accessible place for storing the
files all together, as near to his or her favoured working spot as

possible. Build into the timetable a regular weekly session for sorting loose notes and handouts into files (and filling in gaps and updating work), with you helping out if need be.

Find a competent classmate or two willing to help out

If notes go missing, gaps need to be filled or if homework instructions or materials get forgotten, it is useful for your child to have some classmates to contact for help. If your child doesn't want to ask a friend for help, it might be a good idea to ask a teacher to make an arrangement that works.

Encourage making lists regularly

Get your child to make lists of things to do and tick items off as they are done. Lists are especially easy to update and revise throughout the day if they are in the school diary (or another portable system if there is insufficient space in the diary). Post-Its, of a size that fits into the diary, can be helpful disposable reminders for the forgetful. Care needs to be taken to help your child avoid losing the school diary – either it goes in a pocket or in the school bag – and it helps to have some morning and evening checking system to make sure the diary is where it should be.

BANISH 'LAZINESS' AND GET MOTIVATED

Children who turn out to have a specific learning difficulty have often, at some point in their school life, been labelled as lazy. The word lazy usually implies 'can't be bothered' or just 'won't do it'. However, children with learning difficulties may experience very strong feelings of failure, low self-worth and frustration because, no matter how hard they try, they just don't seem to get anywhere. So they may stop trying and give up on academic work – actively avoiding hard work, losing books and work on purpose, saying they have no homework, finding excuses for not settling down to do homework or completing class work. This laziness – or, as we see it, the *loss of motivation* – comes from their learning problem. 'Laziness' is not a useful description but 'lack of motivation' is, because it implies that action can be taken to restore it.

Set up a star chart

For **younger children**, a version of a star chart works well (using a variety of stickers or colouring in). To get a system going, decide what the *targets* are that you want your child to achieve. Discuss these with him or her, make them *specific* and write them down. Examples are:

- start homework within 20 minutes of coming home
- have ready all the pencils and books needed to do the homework
- spend one lot of 15 minutes on homework (concentrating)
- write four lines with neat writing

There shouldn't be too many targets at any one time, but they do need to be *clear*. If you give a sticker for 'getting on with it', this won't work in the long term because it is too vague a target. It might be fine for a while until you and your child start to disagree (for example, your child claims to be working because he or she is sitting down. You say your child is daydreaming and hasn't written anything). At this point, some children will refuse to go along with the system at all. Don't let this happen!

Draw up a *chart* to record your child's *successes*. This can be a straightforward chart like the example opposite, or it can be a picture with squares drawn in it, such as a guitar for a child who likes music and wants to save up for lessons or CDs, or a book for a child who wants to save for a new book – let your imagination roam freely. Whatever the form of the chart, the spaces can be coloured in or have stickers posted in them. Make sure the wording sounds positive (for example, 'working or concentrating well' rather than 'working without messing around').

	Mon	Tue	Wed	Thur	Fri
Starting work (within 20 minutes)					
Working well on homework (sticker for each 15 minutes)					
Neat writing (parents to decide)					
Remembering to bring work and diary home					

Stick the stickers on *daily* (it is demotivating to forget and get behind). Give *extra stickers for a 'full house'* – that is, if your child succeeds in earning the maximum on any one day, call it a full house and tell your child that he or she is entitled to extra stickers (as a further incentive). Give further bonuses or extra stickers for succeeding for, say, three days in a row (this again gives extra incentive to keep going).

Set up a points system

For **older children and teenagers** a much more sophisticated system is needed to succeed in engaging them. A '*points system*', explained as 'performance-related pay', can be very effective. Points can be added up for specific items the child wants (such as items of clothing, games, comics) or time spent doing things he or she enjoys (such as going to a football match, having a sleepover or having a pizza in front of a DVD).

First, come to an *agreement* with your child about setting up a points system as an incentive to work. There will need to be clear evidence of benefit to your child if the system is to be effective. If your child already receives pocket money 'for free', you may need to negotiate a lower amount – but a chance to earn much more. If your child receives a huge amount of money or treats, a little more or less will make no difference so the incentive to work will be low. The trick is to get the right balance between what you can afford and your child's expectations.

Set out, together, on a piece of paper *exactly what has to be done to earn points*. Keep this paper – your '*rule book*' – to hand. These examples of targets are helpful for most children, but you may need to adapt some or add others for your child:

■ start homework within 25 or 20 minutes of returning home from school (1 point)
■ work for 15 minutes (1 point) but with a bonus for, say, three-quarters of an hour with short breaks in between (4 points)
■ remember to bring home homework diary (1 point)
■ hand in work on time (1 point)
■ complete work in advance (see the Homework Chart details) (number of points given should depend on how quickly the child starts the work, and so on, and should be in the parent's gift – some targets are easy to allocate a fixed amount of points to; others need a more flexible approach)
■ achieve good grades or marks (parents will need to discuss with the child how many points would be fair)
■ file notes at the end of the day or week

Other behavioural targets can also be added to help with setting up routines, such as:

■ packing school/sports bags the night before and placing them by the front door
■ being in bed by …
■ being at breakfast by …
■ being ready to leave the house at …

Make a points chart like the one opposite. Take the targets from the rule book and write a short version on to the chart:

POINTS EARNED FOR	Mon	Tue	Wed	Thur	Fri	Sat	Sun	etc.
Homework started at time agreed								
Work done								
Work done/handed in on time								
Work done in advance								
Good grades/marks								
Points chart filled in								
Bags packed night before								
Up to bed by agreed time								
Ready to leave house by agreed time								
BONUSES FOR: initiative, helpfulness, co-operation, not responding to provocation and so on								
TOTALS: DAILY								
WEEKLY								

Note that there is a space at the end of the targets for additional opportunities to earn bonuses. This gives your child the chance to earn important extra bonus points that come from parents noticing *anything good that has been done* such as being helpful, kind to siblings, patient in the face of provocation and frustration; getting on with work despite being ill or tired; tidying up after him/herself; showing initiative – and so on. The number of points awarded should be in the parent's gift. This part of the scheme provides a positive way of encouraging good habits and values over the longer term.

If your child manages to get the maximum score on any target for, say, three days in a row, add a bonus point (or points) on the third day. Write the bonus points down in the form of +1 (or + however many points are appropriate) so it is clear that the extra point(s) are bonuses. The idea of this is to build in incentives to keep going week by week – otherwise the risk is that all goes well for the first week and then your child loses interest.

Making the points system work

How the points system is carried out is extremely important. Here are some tips to help:

■ The points need to be *added up daily* so none are forgotten, and written into the TOTAL box. A separate WEEKLY TOTAL can also be useful to watch week-by-week progress. If extra bonus points can be earned for 'beating last week's total', the incentive to earn more points should increase.

■ Bedtime is usually the best moment for completing the chart, and if both parents can be on hand to do this and to admire, so much the better.

■ Parents need to *concentrate on praise* for what has been successfully achieved and *not* use this special 'points awarding time' to mention the things that their child failed to do or could have done better.

■ *Points, once earned, should not be removed* – however angry you feel with your child. If you get cross, you risk your child rejecting the scheme altogether. Try not to feel, as some parents occasionally do, that your child should not be given rewards for things you feel he or she is supposed to do as a matter of routine.

■ Make sure that you *constantly build in new incentives*, such as looking for new rewards or changing the look or layout of the charts to make them more exciting.

■ In the school holidays many children like to continue some form of earning incentives; in absence of homework you could give points for, say, reading books, double points for any time spent on school work/projects, sorting out their bedroom and files, and so on.

Set up a thermometer chart

This is the chart – like a 'roof appeal' – to collect up the points your child has earned and display them in an easy-to-view way. The number of points earned each week can be shown by lightly colouring in part of the column. The points spent (on a reward) can be shown by cross-hatching. This will make it clear to parent and child how many points have been earned in total, how many have been spent, and how many are still left to spend.

Thermometer charts can be made in any shape, if your child prefers – for example, in the shape of the object being saved up for. You simply have to draw the shape and draw inside it a grid of squares, each of which equates to one point.

To make the thermometer chart as effective as possible, add in the points earned on a regular basis – daily or once a week. Decide on a target number of points for the top of the chart. This will depend on the age of your child and roughly how many points might be earned as a maximum in any one week (which in turn depends on how many target behaviours you have chosen for your child to be working on). As a rule of thumb, the younger the child, the shorter the possible waiting time to achieve rewards should be. So, if your child wants to save up for something, it

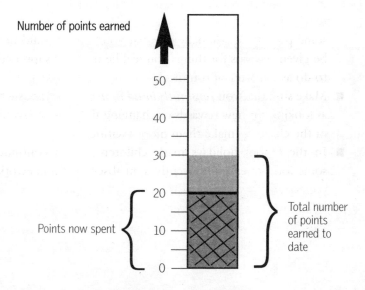

should not be too big but manageable in around three weeks. If your child insists on something big, perhaps mini-rewards can be given along the way for, say, every 20 points earned. A dip into a 'lucky dip' of pre-wrapped small treats or some special stickers might do the trick. Parents should not hand out lots of big treats. Most children will lose the incentive to make an effort if the goodies come too easily. Teenagers and some older children might like to have two charts going – one for saving up for something big that they are prepared to wait a while for, and a second to provide an instant source of pocket money for them to spend (more or less!) as they please. For something saved up for over a very long period it would be reasonable for parents to add in something 'for free' (equivalent to interest in a savings account).

You cannot keep going indefinitely with thermometer charts and points schemes. However, because a systematic reward scheme – including 'performance-related pay' – instead of parental despair and nagging is such a powerful tool, it's good to keep coming back to it throughout the school years. Of course there will need to be changes to suit the child's age as well as breaks from schemes on a regular basis, but if you can find inventive and new ways to make everything interesting and of value to your child, you will have a useful way of helping your child forwards in many areas of education and behaviour.

■   ■   ■

Get yourself and your child into good habits. Routines help homework, and good homework habits put less stress and strain on all the family. A relaxed but systematic approach to revision and taking exams will help further, and use rewards to keep motivation going.

Finally, keep a sense of perspective – don't let your child's learning difficulties take over your or any of your children's lives. Keep a sense of humour about it. There's no harm in making an occasional joke about your child's spelling errors for instance, as long as he or she can laugh over them with you, and doesn't feel laughed at.

Appendix: Felix

Finally ... what of the future? We end this book, as we started, with a real story. This is the story of Helen's own son, Felix.

Felix, now 17, is still at school (and beginning his sixth form years). This is the story of what it has been like for him to have dyspraxia (and mild dyslexia).

Felix's story (as told to Valerie)

I don't remember much about my first assessment, but I do remember becoming aware that I was dyspraxic when I was still at primary school. The things I've found hardest have been organising myself, reading my own handwriting and managing to get things done in time. Some subjects have been especially hard for me – like understanding geometry, drawing straight lines, colouring in and labelling maps and science drawings, and keeping my work clean and tidy. My teachers have been very supportive and my friends know I have difficulties. The extra time in exams has been a big help. And my friends have been great – tying my shoelaces for sports even when I was 11, and letting me have their class notes when I'd lost or couldn't read my own.

I've been grateful for the support my parents have given me. The strategies my mum talked me through have been a great help, though some of the micromanagement is not always welcome. My dad teases me about being dyspraxic when my drawings are rubbish. But I don't mind! It doesn't worry me being dyspraxic and I'm not embarrassed to talk about it.

Valerie asked me what my greatest achievements have been so far. I was pleased with my GCSE results, though maybe English was a little disappointing. I had to work especially hard to practise the maths and science with my mum – but it paid off. My other great achievement is my violin playing, which I want to continue after I've left school. It took me longer to get my body position right when I first learned to play, and learning to read music wasn't easy. But practise got me there in the end. It's something I really enjoy and it's helped me a lot with my co-ordination, my concentration and my time management.

What are *my* top tips?

- Learning to use a multisensory approach to learning facts – so writing down words, saying letters as you write them, recording hard words on an audiotape and playing them back.
- Getting round handwriting problems by learning to touch type and using the laptop for coursework, essays and exams.
- Revising for exams in small 15-minute chunks and using a timer so as not to get distracted by constantly looking at a clock.
- Setting up routines and timetables so that you don't leave things until the last minute.

Valerie asked me what I need to do more of. I'd say I need to use lists more, ticking the items off as I work through them – I'm still not very good at this.

Organisations and Resources

Useful organisations

Dyslexia Action: Park House, Wick Rd, Egham, Surrey TW20 0HH (tel: 01784 222300; www.dyslexiaaction.org.uk; e-mail – info@dyslexiaaction.org.uk)
Head office of national organisation offering assessments and specialist teaching for children and adults with dyslexia at centres around the UK.

British Dyslexia Association: (www.bdadyslexia.org.uk; national helpline 0845 251 9002).
A national organisation offering support and advice for individuals with dyslexia. Regional organisations spread throughout the UK give advice on local resources, including specialist teachers.

The Dyspraxia Foundation: (www.dyspraxiafoundation.org.uk; tel: 01462 454986)
An organisation with a network of local groups offering parents and teachers advice on how children with dyspraxia (DCD) can be supported.

Association for all Speech Impaired Children (AFASIC): (www.afasic.org.uk; tel: 0845 355 5577)
A support and advisory charity for families and professionals caring for children with diagnosed speech and language impairments.

Attention Deficit Disorder Information and Support Services (ADDISS): (www.addiss.co.uk; tel: 020 8906 9068)
ADHD UK Alliance: (www.adhdalliance.org.uk; tel: 0808 808 3555)
These organisations for parents, groups and professionals aim to raise awareness of, and support for, individuals with ADHD.

CReSTeD (Council for the Registration of Schools Teaching Dyslexic Pupils): (www.crested.org.uk; tel: 01242 604 852)
Gives details of independent schools that offer a range of different levels of specialist support for children with specific learning difficulties.

Professional Association for Teachers of Students with Specific Learning Difficulties (PATOSS): (www.patoss-dyslexia.org; tel: 01386 712 650)
Another very helpful organisation which gives details of qualified specialist teachers throughout the UK.

Royal College of Speech and Language Therapists: (www.rcslt.org; tel: 020 7378 1200)
Provides lists of independent speech and language therapists throughout the UK.

Resources

Barrington Stoke Children's Publishers: (www.barrington-stoke.co.uk; tel: 0131 225 4113)
Offers an excellent range of books specially written for children with dyslexia (particularly for children with a reading age of six and a half but an interest age of 10–13 years; reading age seven but with an interest age of 8–12 and 12–16; and for those with a reading age of eight there are several series of books going up to the late teens).

Waterstone's Guide to Books for Young Dyslexic Readers
Produced in association with Dyslexia Action, this wide range of books is sorted in a very helpful and systematic way, providing

reading ages to help parents select books of a suitable level for their child.

Listening Books: (www.listening-books.org.uk; tel: 020 7407 9417; membership@listening-books.org.uk)
Offers a huge range of books on audiotapes, covering fiction and factual subjects useful for school learning. It is a postal and Internet-based membership library service open to children and adults with any kind of special needs that affect reading or holding a book. Also available are MP3 CDs and Internet streaming.

ACE (Aurally Coded English) Spelling Dictionary: LDA Publishers, 1996
An easy-to-use dictionary designed for children of all ages (and adults) who need help with spelling.

Centre for Reading and Language, University of York: (www.york.ac.uk/res/crl)
To find out more about reading, language and dyslexia.

Dealing with Dyscalculia by Steve Chinn gives excellent ideas for dealing with specific topics in maths, including percentages, measuring, probability, time and clocks, averages and angles (see Bibliography).

Kumon Maths: (www.kumon.co.uk; tel: 0800 854 714)
After-school study programmes for children of all ages (see page 193).

Addacus Ltd: (www.addacus.co.uk; tel: 01943 871902)
Graded number programmes with attractive materials covering a wide range of maths topics, and with teacher as well as parent packages.

Wordshark and *Numbershark*: published by White Space Ltd (www.wordshark.co.uk; tel: 020 8748 5927)
Recommended by the BDA for helping children with dyslexia

and for those with maths difficulties. Wordshark is a series of graded phonic games for primary and secondary school level, covering phonemes, words and sentences, and is based on the dyslexia teaching package Alpha to Omega. Numbershark, for children aged 6–14 years, is a graded structured course to help understanding and memorising of number facts and procedures.

Inclusive Technology: (www.inclusive.co.uk; tel: 01457 819790)
Offers a wide range of educational software, including some good programs for children with dyslexia or maths problems (we especially liked Alphabet Track, Phoneme Track, Word Track, Spell Track and Number Track).

Touch-type Read and Spell: (Head Office tel: 020 8464 1330; www.ttrs.co.uk)
Very good systematic typing course based on the Alpha to Omega reading and spelling programme. There are many centres throughout the UK.

Iansyst Software Products: (www.iansyst.co.uk; www.dyslexic. com)
Offer a wide range of software suitable for children with specific learning difficulties as well as portable spelling devices and audio note-takers. We especially liked their touch-typing software for children of eight years and over called Nessy Fingers (www.nessy. com). Some of the spelling programs are worth looking at too, as is Clicker Phonics.

The Left-Handed Shop: (www.anythinglefthanded.co.uk; tel: 020 8770 3722)
Offers a wide range of materials, including special pens, for the left-handed.

Centre for Working Memory and Learning, University of York: (www.york.ac.uk/res/wml)
To find out how working memory difficulties affect learning in the classroom.

Learning Development Aids (LDA): (www.ldalearning.com; tel: 0845 1204 776)
Offers a huge range of teaching materials covering language, literacy, mathematics and writing skills (including phonics games, pencil grips and reading comprehension materials).

www.schoolzone.co.uk/resources/evaluations
You can get independent reviews of software from this organisation, which has been set up by the Department for Children, Schools and Families (formerly DfES).

Bibliography

Chinn, S. *Dealing with Dyscalculia*, London, Souvenir Press, 2007
Doyle, J. *Dyslexia: An Introductory Guide*, London, Whurr Publishers, 1996
Muter, V. *Early Reading Development and Dyslexia*, London, Whurr Publishers, 2003
Taylor, Professor E. *Understanding Your Hyperactive Child*, London, Vermilion, 1985–97
Taylor, J. *Handwriting: A Teacher's Guide*, London, Fulton Publishers, 2001

Index